Delphi Programming Projects

Build a range of exciting projects by exploring cross-platform development and microservices

William Duarte

BIRMINGHAM - MUMBAI

Delphi Programming Projects

Commissioning Editor: Richa Tripathi
Acquisition Editor: Shriram Shekhar
Content Development Editor: Akshita Billava
Technical Editors: Sabaah Navlekar and Mayank Dubey
Copy Editor: Safis Editing
Project Coordinator: Prajakta Naik
Proofreader: Safis Editing
Indexer: Pratik Shirodkar
Graphics: Tom Scaria
Production Coordinator: Deepika Naik

First published: May 2019

Production reference: 1020519

Published by Packt Publishing Ltd.
Livery Place
35 Livery Street
Birmingham
B3 2PB, UK.

ISBN 978-1-78913-055-3

www.packtpub.com

I dedicate this book to God, who allowed me to write it.
To my mother, Sandra, who made me who I am today, and to the memory of my father, Jorge, the best father I could have had.
For the love of my life, my wife, Aline Duarte—thank you for bringing me back to life!
And no less important, my beloved son, Guilherme, you help me to move on! I love you very much, my son!

-William Duarte

`mapt.io`

Mapt is an online digital library that gives you full access to over 5,000 books and videos, as well as industry leading tools to help you plan your personal development and advance your career. For more information, please visit our website.

Why subscribe?

- Spend less time learning and more time coding with practical eBooks and Videos from over 4,000 industry professionals

- Improve your learning with Skill Plans built especially for you

- Get a free eBook or video every month

- Mapt is fully searchable

- Copy and paste, print, and bookmark content

Packt.com

Did you know that Packt offers eBook versions of every book published, with PDF and ePub files available? You can upgrade to the eBook version at `www.packt.com` and as a print book customer, you are entitled to a discount on the eBook copy. Get in touch with us at `customercare@packtpub.com` for more details.

At `www.packt.com`, you can also read a collection of free technical articles, sign up for a range of free newsletters, and receive exclusive discounts and offers on Packt books and eBooks.

Foreword

Programming can be difficult, especially when you have a challenging project. Therefore, when this project is crucial to someone's business, being the right programmer is a gift to your sponsor. As a business owner, as well as a programmer myself, I can surely say that William Duarte is this kind of blessed programmer we rarely find.

Some years ago, I needed to change the **enterprise resource planning** (**ERP**) of my company, on account of the strict Brazilian fiscal regulations. At that time, we had a fully internally developed, private label credit card. It was mandatory that it worked in a totally new environment, seamlessly integrating with a new **point-of-sale** (**POS**) system. Following two years of trial and error, of using the services of huge consultancy firms and wasting a lot of money, I was about to give up. That is when I met William Duarte.

In a casual meeting with Mr. Duarte's former employer, I told him about the difficulties in getting our credit card system to operate properly. He introduced me to William, who, in a quick chat, told me he was quite confident that not only could he do what I needed, but he could do it fast. In total disbelief, I asked him to prove it and he just smiled and said: *"Fine! I can make it work in a test environment in a couple of weeks. Just wait and see."* I felt like laughing when I heard that. How could someone do something that a whole team of programmers couldn't do—and in a matter of weeks, not months? *"He will never do it,"* I thought. However, to my surprise, he did it. The test was a success; thus, I quickly signed a contract with his former company. Nowadays, my credit card system is up and running perfectly, and, fortunately, William Duarte works for me.

If you need to improve your Delphi programming performance, I strongly feel that William can help you with this task. You are in good hands. I have witnessed countless times William's skills and how useful good Delphi programming is for real-life challenges. Therefore, if you are seeking a solid foundation for successful Delphi projects, the hunt is over.

Enjoy your reading!

Rafael Sampaio

Retail executive and owner of Impecável Roupas, a Brazilian chain of stores.

Rio de Janeiro, Brazil

I met William at the annual Embarcadero Conference in Brazil where he was signing copies of one of his previous books. He gave me a copy, but unfortunately, I don't read Portuguese, but I appreciated the book, and luckily, source code is the universal language. He and I became friends, and I was happy to have his expertise and enthusiasm as part of the Embarcadero MVP Program. Most recently, he became an MVP Regional Coordinator for Brazil.

I like the project-oriented nature of this book. It tackles different types of projects with different technologies, such as in the first chapter, where it shows how to capture images, apply filters, and share the images. This is common functionality in many social media applications, and something that Delphi makes easy. I frequently use the basics of this as a quick demo when introducing someone to Delphi's productivity.

The REST client functionality is another favorite feature of mine. I spend a lot of time, as I'm sure most developers do, integrating with web services all over the web. Delphi's REST client library makes it easy to connect to these services and work with the data in your applications. Beyond the REST client library that comes with Delphi, there are numerous specialized REST components, including the Enterprise Connectors and the TMS Web Controls Pack, which are turnkey options for connecting to many different individual web services.

Database access is something that was a key component of the very first release of Delphi. While it isn't, strictly speaking, part of the language, having good database connectivity is part of what defines Delphi. The new FireDAC database access framework is simply amazing. I seriously wish it was part of Delphi years ago, when I was doing more database development. So, be sure you check out William's chapter on databases!

I've said it before, but it continues to be more and more true—it is a great time to be a Delphi developer, especially when you have a copy of a great book on Delphi projects, like this one!

Jim McKeeth

Chief Developer Advocate for Embarcadero Technologies.

Nampa, Idaho, USA

Contributors

About the author

William Duarte is a Delphi Certified Developer and Embarcadero Regional MVP Coordinator. He began his career in 2005 as a programmer. He was recognized as an internationally certified Retail Technical Consultant by Retail Pro in 2007. He is a specialist in commercial automation and desktop/mobile development, and the author of a book in Portuguese—*Delphi for Android and iOS*, by *Brasport*, 2015. He is currently working as a consultant for the Brazilian Navy and retail chain stores.

About the reviewer

André Luis Celestino is a Senior Delphi Developer with more than seven years' experience in the software development field. He is a Certified Delphi Developer, SAFe Practitioner, and Embarcadero MVP since 2017. He also has a postgraduate qualification in software engineering, with an emphasis on Agile methodologies. He is currently working as a Senior Delphi Developer at DB1 Global Software, a Brazilian software development company.

I would like to thank my wife, Beatriz, and my daughter, Leticia, for all their support, love, and understanding during the process of reviewing this book.

I would also like to thank DB1 Global Software for all the knowledge and confidence acquired there. It is a fantastic company with amazing people.

Packt is searching for authors like you

If you're interested in becoming an author for Packt, please visit `authors.packtpub.com` and apply today. We have worked with thousands of developers and tech professionals, just like you, to help them share their insight with the global tech community. You can make a general application, apply for a specific hot topic that we are recruiting an author for, or submit your own idea.

Table of Contents

Preface

Delphi is a cross-platform programming language that supports rapid application development for Microsoft Windows, Apple Mac OS X, Android, and iOS and Linux (server-side). This book consists of seven independent projects that will help you upgrade your Delphi programming skills and guide you through best practices, design patterns, RTL resources, and more.

You will learn how to build responsive user interfaces for desktop and mobile with FireMonkey and implement a microservices architecture using the **Rapid Application Development (RAD)** server. You will also create clones of popular applications such as Instagram and Facebook using Delphi 10.3, and learn the principles of clean code to master Delphi.

Who this book is for

This book is for developers, programmers, and IT professionals who want to learn the best market practices by implementing practical projects. It is important to have prior knowledge of the Delphi language.

What this book covers

Chapter 1, *Building an Instagram Clone*, introduces the basics of layouts and responsiveness on Android and iOS platforms and also how to use SVG icons, camera features, permissions, and a mobile device's media library.

Chapter 2, *Building a Facebook REST API*, deals with building an application that consumes the Facebook REST API using native REST components and working with JSON.

Chapter 3, *Cross-Platform Services for Windows, iOS, and Android*, covers how service applications take requests from client applications, process those requests, and return information to client applications. It also covers how they typically run in the background, without much user input.

Chapter 4, *Design Patterns to Build a Multi-Database System*, deals with design patterns such as singleton, repository, and others for creating multi-database applications and isolating business rules from forms.

Chapter 5, *Creating GUI Apps with FireMonkey*, introduces the concepts of Material Design and simulates the use of Material Design using FireMonkey visual components.

Chapter 6, *Implementing Tethering to Create a Remote Control*, introduces app-tethering technology, and how to turn a mobile device into a remote control for a computer (using Wi-Fi or Bluetooth connections).

Chapter 7, *Building Microservices Using the RAD Server*, shows how to develop microservices architecture implement it in Delphi, and use a non-centralized architecture, where we can perform different functions on different platforms.

To get the most out of this book

To get the most out of this book, readers should be experienced programmers. You do not necessarily have to be an expert in Delphi, however, basic knowledge of functions, procedures, classes, objects, and databases is required.

It is necessary that, besides Delphi, you have internet access to perform the exercises that appear in some chapters. It is important that you have a physical Android device to hand for testing.

Download the example code files

You can download the example code files for this book from your account at www.packt.com. If you purchased this book elsewhere, you can visit www.packt.com/support and register to have the files emailed directly to you.

You can download the code files by following these steps:

1. Log in or register at www.packt.com.
2. Select the **SUPPORT** tab.
3. Click on **Code Downloads & Errata**.
4. Enter the name of the book in the **Search** box and follow the onscreen instructions.

Once the file is downloaded, please make sure that you unzip or extract the folder using the latest version of:

- WinRAR/7-Zip for Windows
- Zipeg/iZip/UnRarX for Mac
- 7-Zip/PeaZip for Linux

The code bundle for the book is also hosted on GitHub at `https://github.com/PacktPublishing/Delphi-Programming-Projects`. In case there's an update to the code, it will be updated on the existing GitHub repository.

We also have other code bundles from our rich catalog of books and videos available at `https://github.com/PacktPublishing/`. Check them out!

Download the color images

We also provide a PDF file that has color images of the screenshots/diagrams used in this book. You can download it here: `https://www.packtpub.com/sites/default/files/downloads/9781789130553_ColorImages.pdf`.

Conventions used

There are a number of text conventions used throughout this book.

`CodeInText`: Indicates code words in text, database table names, folder names, filenames, file extensions, pathnames, dummy URLs, user input, and Twitter handles. Here is an example: "When you work with a different view of the master, Delphi will create a new `.FMX` file in your project folder. This file will contain the positions of the components for that particular screen format."

A block of code is set as follows:

```
procedure TForm1.DoDidFinish(Image: TBitmap);
begin
  ImgInsta.Bitmap.Assign(Image);
end;
```

When we wish to draw your attention to a particular part of a code block, the relevant lines or items are set in bold:

```
uses REST.Utils,
System.NetEncoding,Web.HTTPApp,System.Net.HttpClient,IdHTTP, uFrmLogin;
```

Any command-line input or output is written as follows:

```
net start PacktBooks_Service
```

Bold: Indicates a new term, an important word, or words that you see onscreen. For example, words in menus or dialog boxes appear in the text like this. Here is an example: "Open the Delphi IDE and create a **Multi-Device Application**. Note that there is the concept of viewing for different screen types."

Warnings or important notes appear like this.

Tips and tricks appear like this.

Get in touch

Feedback from our readers is always welcome.

General feedback: If you have questions about any aspect of this book, mention the book title in the subject of your message and email us at customercare@packtpub.com.

Errata: Although we have taken every care to ensure the accuracy of our content, mistakes do happen. If you have found a mistake in this book, we would be grateful if you would report this to us. Please visit www.packt.com/submit-errata, selecting your book, clicking on the Errata Submission Form link, and entering the details.

Piracy: If you come across any illegal copies of our works in any form on the Internet, we would be grateful if you would provide us with the location address or website name. Please contact us at copyright@packt.com with a link to the material.

If you are interested in becoming an author: If there is a topic that you have expertise in and you are interested in either writing or contributing to a book, please visit authors.packtpub.com.

Reviews

Please leave a review. Once you have read and used this book, why not leave a review on the site that you purchased it from? Potential readers can then see and use your unbiased opinion to make purchase decisions, we at Packt can understand what you think about our products, and our authors can see your feedback on their book. Thank you!

For more information about Packt, please visit `packt.com`.

Building an Instagram Clone 1

The world has changed. We are in the new digital age where, every day, more and more apps are available to the users. So, what really grabs attention, since we have so many options available? Features, user experience, rich design? We can say that, with Delphi, we have all the ability to develop rich applications, both graphically and in terms of functionality.

A major challenge for Delphi developers is the paradigm shift between desktop and mobile platforms. The way to develop and draw a form is different, of course; however, many developers program as if they were still working with a Delphi 7 IDE.

If you are this type of developer and want to learn more about responsive design and how to change your desktop mindset for mobile, then this is an ideal chapter for you.

We have chosen an application already on the market—Instagram—to better elucidate these insights and this paradigm shift.

In this Delphi version of Instagram, you will be introduced to the following topics:

- Mindset between desktop and mobile
- Creating responsive layouts
- Creating buttons with **Scalable Vector Graphics** (**SVG**) icons
- Interacting with the camera
- Sharing photos

The knowledge necessary for understanding this chapter is basic. Experience with Delphi is not necessary; minimal knowledge of the IDE and some components, such as buttons, edits, and list views, is sufficient.

Technical requirements

To get started, you must have a version of Delphi installed on your computer. For the examples, we will use Delphi Rio, but you can use your version of Delphi, provided it is from Seattle 10 or later.

The code files for this chapter are present on GitHub at `https://github.com/ PacktPublishing/Delphi-Programming-Projects/tree/master/Chapter01`.

Project overview

The goal of this project is to enable you to better understand the use of visual components and the concept of responsive design, and introduce the concepts of actions and use them to take beautiful photos.

The estimated build time is two to five minutes.

Getting started

It is necessary to have access to the internet to access sites that offer SVG.

No download is required.

Mindset difference between desktop and mobile

When smartphones became essential and the emergence of the three major mobile OS competitors (iOS, Android, and Windows phone—this last one has been discontinued) took shape, developers were confused. After all, who was not accustomed to responsiveness or smaller screens? Before diving into this new world, you need to understand some important things.

Developing for the Windows desktop, we have some benefits—available memory, ease of interface design (usually in resolutions of at least 1,024 x 768), and others. Most of these features make the programmer's life much more focused on the logic of the application without worrying too much about available computer resources or the like.

When web applications began to emerge with their HTTP protocol in the best request-response style, a new concept of development was created. The programmer had to adapt to the new markup languages (HTML and CSS) and had to separate their application in what we call the server/client side. So, anyone who previously programmed into a single programming language (such as Java or C#) had to adapt to learn markup languages. And, with a need for insertion in the web world, the programmer needed to deal with screen sizes. On the other hand, the applications should be more and more responsive to work more in the varied sizes of screen, from tiny phones to tablets and desktops; not to mention the limitations of the hardware, since they have less processing power and memory than desktop computers.

Mobile has combined the advantages of the previous two along with their disadvantages. If it was said in the web application that everything was on the web, that is to say, for any user access just entering the site, the mobile brought back the desktop concept. The application is installed in the device, and, if you have to upgrade the application, you have to do so for each device. We return to the same situation as desktop applications.

Having limited hardware, including reduced screen size and the absence of peripherals means that the challenge for the mobile developer is more complex

Before you start reading into this topic, you must abandon certain preconceptions, such as the idea that developing for mobile is the same as doing so for web or desktop. No, it's not! Remember that your user is on a limited device and does not have any peripherals for assistance, such as a mouse or keyboard.

Follow these steps to learn about viewing for different screen types:

1. Open the Delphi IDE and create a **Multi-Device Application.** Note that different screen types will have different viewing characteristics:

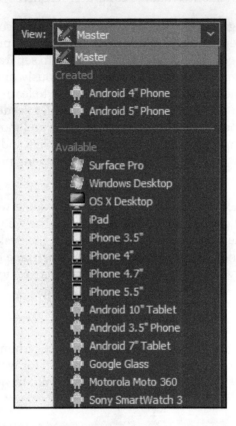

2. Select one Android or iPhone view.

 Note that the display format is changed. Try working on master view and switch views to keep track of the layout of your components on the form.

When you work with a different view of the master, Delphi will create a new `.FMX` file in your project folder. This file will contain the positions of the components for that particular screen format. The paradigm shift is not just about the size or the screen format, but the Delphi IDE helps us identify those nuances.

Range of sizes

There are a range of sizes used to determine the view that is used in Android apps. Note that the runtime does not require an exact match to select a view. The runtime chooses the closest match. The following table shows the ranges for each view, specified in landscape coordinates:

View Name	Minimum Size (Pixels)	Maximum Size (Pixels)	PPI
Android 3.5" Phone	800x500	1,000x600	320
Android 4" Phone	1,1168x730	1,360x850	320
Android 5" Phone	1440x900	1,708x960	320
Android 7" Tablet	1708x960	1,920x1,200	320
Android 10" Tablet	2,400x1,500	2,560x1,600	320

It is possible to visualize the layout of the forms in the device in real time by looking at the Berlin version design time. Fantastic, isn't it? To do this, download the Fire UI Live Preview application from your platform store (Google Play: `http://docwiki.embarcadero.com/RADStudio/Rio/en/FireUI_App_Preview`, or Apple Store: `https://itunes.apple.com/us/app/fireui-app-preview-10.1-berlin/id1090861997`) or install directly via the `C:\Program Files (x86)\Embarcadero\Studio\20.0\LivePreview\` path.

FireUI Live Preview is a server/client multi-device tool that allows you to broadcast the active form of your application, in real time, to several devices simultaneously.

Creating responsive layouts

In this topic, you will learn how to work with responsive layouts in Delphi using **FireMonkey (FMX)**. For the examples, we will use Delphi Tokyo. Let's have a look at the required steps:

1. To start, open Delphi and create a new project by navigating to **File | New | Multi-Device Application-Delphi** and select **Blank Application**:

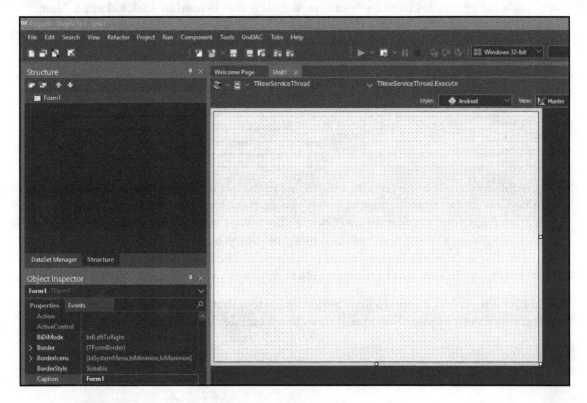

Adjust the style for Android; for example, for the view, we will continue in the **Master** view.

Give preference to working in the **Master** view. During development, if you want to modify views and add new controls to your form, the responsiveness properties will not be inherited. For example, when adding a **TButton** component to a 4-inch Android view, properties will be lost if you create to modify for a different view, such as iPhone. In the **Master** view, all the characteristics will be kept, keeping their proportions clear, by the platform.

2. Add a **Toolbar** component to your form.
3. Create two buttons inside **Toolbar**.
4. Select the two buttons and align to the left.
5. Modify the margins to 5 on each property.
6. Save your project and run the application for a Windows platform.
7. Then, select the first button that is already configured and modify the **StyleLookup** property by selecting the **cameratoolbutton** option. Notice that the button icon is then changed to a specific camera icon.
8. Add another **Toolbar** component, but leave it with bottom alignment. In this toolbar, add a button, align it to the right, and change its margins to 5, as in the top buttons. This button will exit the application.
9. Finally, add a **TLayout** component to the center of your form so that it fills the empty area and align it when using **Client**.
10. Also, modify **StyleLookup** for the missing buttons. For the button next to the camera, select **searchtoolbutton**, because, through this, we will search the already-saved images in the device. For the last button, select **escapetoolbutton** in the **StyleLookup** property, because, with this button, we will leave the application.

TLayout

The FireMonkey components have an owner, parent, and children. If you put any component on a form, it becomes the owner and parent of the component.

Using properties such as **Position**, **Align**, **Margins**, and **Padding** with anchors, you will turn your app in to a responsive application.

Note that, even if you resize the form, the buttons remain aligned to the left, respecting the margins, and are inside the toolbar.

FireMonkey layouts are containers for other graphics objects that can be used to build elegant-looking forms. FireMonkey layouts extend the functionality of the controls for the arrangement and scaling of controls.

To achieve rich interfaces using **TLayout**, use more than one layout and the organization properties of the child controls in the layouts.

If everything went well here, you will have a form as shown in the following screenshot:

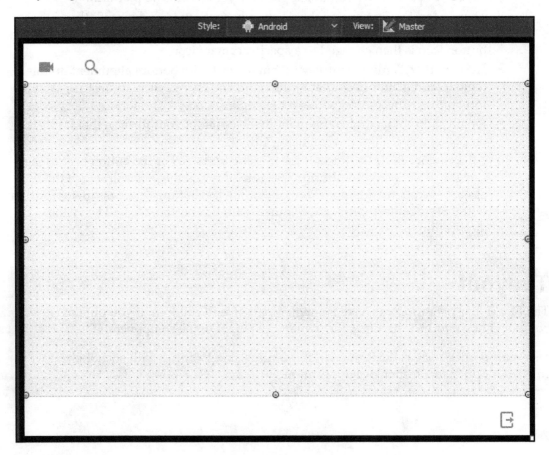

Try creating new views and see the resulting alignment. This is the basic principle for developing a responsive application in FireMonkey.

If you want to view the format with the screen rotated, there is a button to rotate the screen. With this, you can view the layout on the screen in a different format as shown in the following screenshot:

Look at the different types of layouts and their characteristics. For project types where you need to insert many components, use the **ScrollBox** so you can have a scrolling effect on your form.

Creating buttons with SVG icons

In the previous project, we created the main basic layout. Later on, we created photo and sharing events. In this project, we will work with the use of SVG icons, which are infinitely smaller in size in relation to the allocation of space.

SVG is an XML-based vector graphics format that can scale to any size without losing clarity. SVG images and their characteristics are defined in XML text files. That is, they can be searched, indexed, scripted, and compressed. Like XML files, SVG images can be produced and modified with any editing software.

We will use 100% native components in order to use an SVG image. To do this, follow this step by step:

1. From the **Tool Pallet**, select **TRectangle**. Add in the toolbar created previously, use the property, and align the rectangle by setting it to the center. You will now have a rectangle centered in the toolbar.
2. Add a speed button inside this same rectangle. Note that in the **Structure** pane, the button is contained within the shape. Do the same with the **TPath** component, but leave it as the child of the speed button. Align both to **Center**.
3. Clear the **Text** property of the new speed button:

The structure of your application should be like this, with the components nested.

4. Okay, now that you have the basic structure assembled on your form, it's time to choose an SVG icon to illustrate this button. The purpose of this button is to execute the share function when clicked. So, we can now share a photo. You can search the internet for various SVG icons. In this example, you can copy the SVG code at http://materialdesignicons.com/ to use in our application.

5. The icon used is Instagram. It is important to note that in certain tools or websites, such as `materialdesignicons.com`, you have the functionality to view the SVG code and also to be able to download the binary file. A simpler way to get the SVG code is to view it online:

In this case, to copy the correct information from the SVG vector, go directly to the `d=` property and copy its content. This property contains the icon code:

6. Once you have the content of the SVG vector, you can include it in your Delphi application using the **TPath** component. To do so, follow these steps:
    1. Select the **TPath** component.
    2. Select the **Data** property.
    3. Input the SVG content and save as shown in the following screenshot:

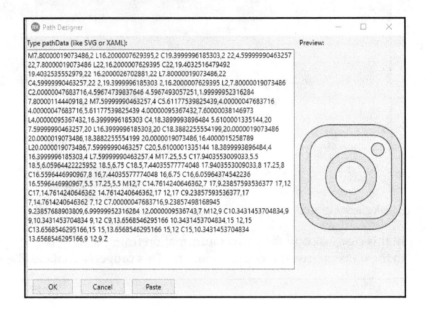

 Note that by entering the content of the data tag in the **TPath** component, you can preview the image.

This is what the Instagram icon looks like:

You can color the icon in the **Fill** property, including **Gradient**. To remove the border, just leave it as **None** in the **Stroke.Kind** property at **Object Inspector**:

 You can also change the color of your button as long as it is inside the rectangle. To do this, change the **Fill.Color** property of the rectangle and watch the magic happen.

In the first two steps, we created a new button and centered the toolbar. Notice that this button has a new component, the **TPath**. The **TPath** is inside our button. This causes the image, which we copy from the internet appears contained in the component. In steps three, four, and six, we located the SVG icon and copied its content through the d property. With the contents of the image copied, we then go to the **TPath** component, making it display the same icon that was selected, in this case, Instagram.

 If you're not familiar with SVG icons, feel free to browse through a variety of other sources. There are numerous websites for downloading icons in various formats, including SVG.

Interacting with the camera

There are at least two ways to take a picture with FireMonkey—the first, for the lazy, is to use an **ActionList**, linking the action of taking a photo to a visual component, such as a button. In this case, your application will request access to the device's camera application.

The second form, however, gives us more freedom in terms of functionality, using **TCameraComponent**. With it, you can set the resolution, specify the type of camera (front or back) that can be used, choose to use the flash, and you can even create your own flashlight application.

Lights, camera, and action!

Now that we have the main screen properly built with its main components anchored, we can work on the main functionality—recording moments! Using the same project as the previous recipes, we will finally develop the code to capture images:

1. First, add a **TImage** component to your form and set its alignment to **alClient**, filling all layout content. We will use this **TImage** to display the photo. Now, do the same for a non-visual component, called **ActionList**. Enter this into the form. Change the **TImage** property and name it as `ImgInsta`.

2. With the right-click on **ActionList**, open the **ActionList Editor** option. With the keyboard, click *Ctrl + Insert* to open the dialog containing the options; you can also go with the mouse on the **New** button and insert the new action. The action we want is **TTakePhotoFromCameraAction**:

In this project, we will capture the image in two ways, the first with a standard action and the other using the IFMXCameraService interface.

3. Let's create the DoDidFinish procedure:

```
procedure TForm1.DoDidFinish(Image: TBitmap); begin
ImgInsta.Bitmap.Assign(Image); end;
```

4. In this procedure, the image parameter, which will come from the camera, will be assigned to the **TImage** component in our form. Remember to assign this procedure to the **OnDidFinishTaking** event of **TTakePhotoFromCameraAction**:

```
procedure TForm1.TakePhotoFromCameraAction1DidFinishTaking(Image:
TBitmap);
begin
  DoDidFinish(Image);
end;
```

In the next few steps, you will understand why this is redundant.

5. We can create a new default action, which will fetch images already saved in the device library. Repeat the process to add a new action to your **ActionList**; however, this time select the **TTakeFromLibrary** action.

If you want your application to automatically save the pictures taken by a device camera to the device photo library, set the `TCustomTakePhotoAction.NeedSaveToAlbum` property to **True**.

6. When selecting the event of this new action, the code is exactly the same code that was made in **TTakePhotoFromCameraAction**:

```
procedure TForm1.TakePhotoFromLibraryAction1DidFinishTaking(Image:
TBitmap);
begin
  DoDidFinish(Image);
end;
```

Note that since the image comes from a parameter, which comes from the action, it allows you to use exactly the same line of code.

7. Bind the respective actions to their execution buttons:

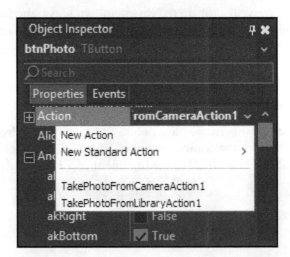

8. Let's increase the project a bit more, including an extra button added to the top in the first toolbar, only this time, right-aligned. This button will also take a picture, but, using the `IFMXCameraService` interface. To perform such an act, include the following units in the `uses` clause of your form:

```
uses
    FMX.MediaLibrary, FMX.Platform, System.Messaging;
```

9. Add another procedure to capture the message coming from the device and thus identify an action to take photos:

```
procedure DoMessageListener(const Sender: TObject; const M:
TMessage);
```

Its implementation is shown in the following code snippet:

```
procedure TForm1.DoMessageListener(const Sender: TObject; const M:
TMessage);
begin
  if M is TMessageDidFinishTakingImageFromLibrary then
ImgInsta.Bitmap.Assign(TMessageDidFinishTakingImageFromLibrary(M).V
alue);
end;
```

10. Encode the `FormCreate` procedure:

```
procedure TForm1.FormCreate(Sender: TObject);
begin
  TMessageManager.DefaultManager.SubscribeToMessage(
    TMessageDidFinishTakingImageFromLibrary, DoMessageListener);
end;
```

11. To conclude, let's encode the **onClick** event of the newly added button:

```
procedure TForm1.Button3Click(Sender: TObject);
var
  Service: IFMXCameraService;
  Params: TParamsPhotoQuery;
begin
  if
TPlatformServices.Current.SupportsPlatformService(IFMXCameraService
,
    Service) then
  begin
    Params.Editable := True;
    // Specifies whether to save a picture to device Photo Library
    Params.NeedSaveToAlbum := True;
    Params.RequiredResolution := TSize.Create(640, 640);
   Params.OnDidFinishTaking := DoDidFinish;
    Service.TakePhoto(Button3, Params);
  end
  else
    ShowMessage('This device does not support the camera service');
end;
```

We divide this project into two parts, where, in the first part, we use an **ActionList** to take a picture. These actions require very little programming; however, they will not work on Windows platforms. In the second part, when using the `IFMXCameraService` interface, we have the freedom to implement our codes with a few more lines but greater freedom. We can also include parameters that allow us to, for example, set the minimum resolution and define whether we will save the image to the device as well.

You should also check the **TCameraComponent** component. You can take your photos without even directing them to your device's camera, including video recordings.

Sharing photos

FireMonkey's basic sharing service does not differ from the way we interact to take a photo; that is, we can use a standard action in our **ActionList1** to create a new event where we share the photo you just took.

Now that our application is responsive and is properly recording the most important moments through photographs, let's share! Using the same example from previous recipes, we will now develop the button event we created with the SVG icon.

The following steps will show you how to share the photos using FireMonkey:

1. Create a new action in the **ActionList1**, in the **Media Library** category, to display the share center. Select the **ShowShareSheetAction1** action:

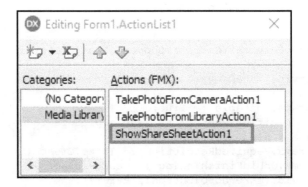

2. The event is now different; in order to share, it is necessary to assign what you want to share. In our project, we will share a photo. For this, we must program the **OnBeforeExecute** event of this action:

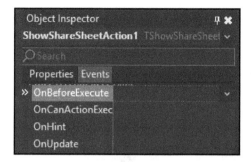

The following is the code for the **OnBeforeExecute** event:

```
procedure TForm1.ShowShareSheetAction1BeforeExecute(Sender:
TObject);
begin
   ShowShareSheetAction1.Bitmap.Assign(ImgInsta.Bitmap);
end;
```

3. Now, to finish, just assign the newly coded action the **Action** property of our button. You can use **Structure** pane and select the **TSpeedButton** (which has the **TPath** component is inside it) component with the Instagram logo. With everything ready, when taking a photo it will be filled through the **TImage** component that can be shared.

The following screenshot shows the form view at development time:

The following screenshot shows the form view running on an Android mobile:

Finally, the application images are still at design time in Delphi and are already running on an Android device.

Summary

We have introduced through this mini Instagram clone how to work with basic responsive design, making sure that, regardless of the size of the screen, our controls adjust according to the screen. Then, through the **TPath** component, we included icons in SVG format, drastically reducing the size of the images and icons thanks to vectorization.

Our code was simple and consisted of only three lines. At a minimum, we can take a photo, choose a photo from the library, and share with friends. All this is done using **ActionList** and interfaces already done in the FireMonkey library.

In the next chapter, you'll be introduced to the wonderful world of APIs. Not only is it possible to consume Facebook API services, but you can develop your application on the platform by interacting with Delphi.

Delphi is this simple, RAD, and practical!

Further reading

For more information, I recommend that you read the official Embarcadero layouts material available at `http://docwiki.embarcadero.com/RADStudio/Rio/en/FireMonkey_Layouts_Strategies`.

Building a Facebook REST API 2

Still talking about social networks, Facebook is undoubtedly the largest one. With more than 2 billion active users in 2018, it had twice the number of users of Instagram and WhatsApp. Curiously, Facebook owns both. Do not be surprised if a new social network belongs to billionaire Mark Zuckerberg.

This chapter will transcend the boundaries of Delphi; you will have to interact with the Facebook platform.

Initially, you will be introduced to Facebook's development platform in order to create an application on the social network. This application will be used to perform the integration between Delphi and Facebook.

You will then learn about **Representational State Transfer** (**REST**) concepts and the **JavaScript Object Notation** (**JSON**) standard. Basically, we will traffic a file or text in JSON format to a REST server, using the Facebook API.

Finally, with a properly configured Facebook application and the REST concepts learned, we will have what we need to do a Facebook login and search for the friends, for example. The possibilities will be according to the permissions that your application needs, from capturing personal information to posting a photo, video, and whatever else the Facebook API allows on the timeline.

Intermediate knowledge is needed to understand this chapter. It is necessary to be well aware of the concepts of web services and security.

In this chapter, you will learn about the following:

- Creating an application on Facebook
- Understanding request and response REST services
- Working with JSON
- Logging in with Facebook

Technical requirements

To get started, you must have a version of Delphi installed on your computer. For the examples, we will use Delphi Rio, but you can use your version of Delphi, provided it is from Seattle 10 or later.

The code files for this chapter are present on GitHub: `https://github.com/ PacktPublishing/Delphi-Programming-Projects/tree/master/Chapter02`.

Facebook Graph API and more

Delphi comes with all the components you need for you to enjoy this chapter. We will basically use the **TRESTClient** component to do this. First, you'll be taught how to authenticate with Facebook and get an access token, and then how to run an Open Graph query to get user information. Being able to authenticate on Facebook is very useful if you are creating any kind of content application for Android or iOS.

The Graph API is the key way to interact with the Facebook platform. It is a low-level API that uses applications to query data, publish new posts, manage ads, upload photos, and more.

Project overview

The purpose of this chapter is to develop a hybrid application (Windows, Android, iOS, and macOS) that will connect to Facebook through the Graph API.

The estimated build time is 10 minutes.

Getting started

You must have internet access to register your application on Facebook and consume the REST API.

Creating an application on Facebook

You need to register your project as an application on Facebook before you can access the Facebook API using Delphi. We can do this using the following page: `https://developers.facebook.com/apps`. The page will look like the following screenshot:

We will create the application on the Facebook platform, which is necessary to perform the integration and log in on the Facebook platform for this project and follow these steps:

1. Add a new application to Facebook. For this chapter, we will call it `DelphiProjectsPackt`:

2. Solve the **reCAPTCHA** and **Submit** your information:

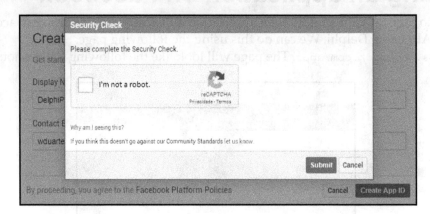

3. Navigate to **Select a Scenario | Integrate Facebook Login**:

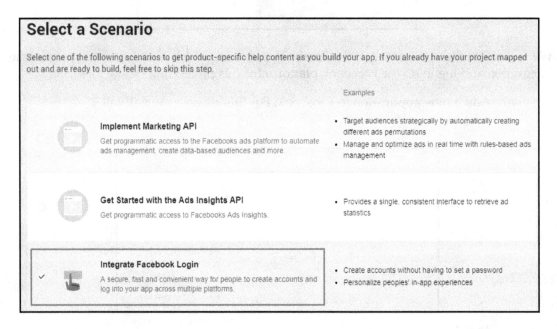

4. Before saving changes, fill in the two required fields—**Privacy Policy URL** and **Category**:

Invalid Privacy Policy URL

You must provide a valid Privacy Policy URL in order take your app Live. Go to Basic Settings and make sure it is valid.

Close

5. Save the changes.
6. Click on **Finish Quickstart**, as shown in the following screenshot:

7. Select **Web** in **Quickstart** options:

8. Confirm the next steps, advancing with the information requested by Facebook.

At this point, it is important that you save the application ID to use later in our Delphi components, in order to access the Facebook platform.

To enable Facebook login in a desktop app, we need to embed a web browser (also referred to as **WebView**) within the app to carry out the login process.

Facebook has several methods for platform access for developers. For mobile devices, it is best to use the SDK. We will use the hybrid model; in this model, you can connect using your desktop application and, including with your mobile application, with FireMonkey.

Let's work on the hybrid model. Try using the official Facebook SDK in your Android and iOS apps. In GitHub, there is a development project called **grijjy**. Check out this link for more information: https://github.com/grijjy/DelphiSocialFrameworks.

It is necessary to initially create an application on the Facebook platform because we need the access token, which will later be your access key to use the Graph API.

Request and response REST services

REST is one of the main models that has been described by Roy Fielding, one of the principal creators of the HTTP protocol, in his Ph.D. thesis and adopted as the model to be used in the evolution of the HTTP protocol architecture.

The Embarcadero REST Library is accessible for all platforms, supported by Delphi.

The framework focuses on JSON as the representation format. The XML format is not supported.

The Embarcadero REST Library consists of three main components—the request, the client, and the response. All are part of a single workflow when submitting, processing, and returning the request with JSON.

TRESTClient

This component performs a request to a REST server. **TRESTClient** manages the HTTP connection to the service, works with HTTP headers, proxy servers, and receives data to be and delivered by **TRESTResponse**.

TRESTRequest

The request contains all the parameters to the request to the current HTTP service. One of the most important properties of the request is the resource. The request also configures HTTP methods (`GET`, `POST`, `PUT`, and `DELETE`) that are used for its execution.

REST.Client.TRESTResponse

The response contains all the service data. The data includes the HTTP request status code, possible error messages, and JSON. The response can be accessed using one of the `Content`, `JSONValue`, or `RAWbytes` properties.

TOAuth2Authenticator

TOAuth2Authenticator implements authentication to OAuth2. This approach will provide specific authorization flows for any application, whether web, desktop, mobile phones, or smart devices. The Facebook Graph API only supports OAuth 2.0.

Get to work (hands-on)

Now that you have the application created on Facebook and understand the basics of REST, open your Delphi, starting a new FireMonkey project, and add the three components of the REST family (client, request, and response), and the OAuth2 component for authentication:

1. Add the **TRestClient** component into your form.
2. Add the **TRestRequest** component into your form.
3. Add the **TRestResponse** component into your form.
4. Add **TOAuth2Authenticator** into your form.
5. Copy the **Accept** property content of **RESTRequest** for **RESTClient**.
6. In **TRestResponse**, put `application/json` in the **Content Type** property.
7. In **TOAuth2Authenticator**:
    1. Change response type to **rtTOKEN**
    2. Put `https://www.facebook.com/dialog/oauth` in the **AuthorizationEndPoint** property
8. In the **Scope** property, put `public_profile.email`.
9. Add two **Edits** for user information.
10. Add a **TCircle** to show a profile photo, named `circle_photo`.
11. Modify the **TCircle Fill.Kind** property: select **Bitmap**.
12. Add a **TButton** for starts events.

Your form should look like this:

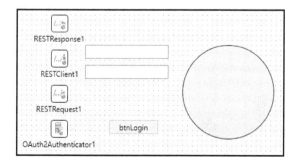

It is important to note that if you do not modify the **Fill.Kind** property of the **TCircle** object, you will not be able to load an image because the expected data type will not be a **Bitmap**.

We have added all the components of the REST triad to access the RESTful Facebook server. The **OAuth2** component is responsible for authenticating our application with the platform. Remember that this is possible because we first created a real application on the Facebook developer platform; without this step, we could not advance.

Text boxes will be used to display the first and last name of the logged-in user and the image to display your profile photo.

For more information about the REST library and how we can consume services with Delphi, access the RESTDEMO sample in `Users\Public\Documents\Embarcadero\Studio\Samples\Object Pascal\Database\RESTDemo\RestDemo.dproj`.

Working with JSON

JSON is an open standard file format that utilizes to convey data objects. These objects consist of attribute-value pairs and array data types. Delphi provides a native library for working with JSON containing classes and methods for storing, parsing, reading, writing, and generating data. Facebook works with JSON information traffic through the Graph API. When you use communication with Facebook's REST server, the expected return is the result of the JSON standard.

The following code snippet illustrates an example in JSON:

```
{
    "glossary": {
        "title": "example glossary",
    "GlossDiv": {
            "title": "S",
      "GlossList": {
                "GlossEntry": {
                    "ID": "SGML",
            "SortAs": "SGML",
            "GlossTerm": "Standard Generalized Markup Language",
            "Acronym": "SGML",
            "Abbrev": "ISO 8879:1986",
            "GlossDef": {
                        "para": "A meta-markup language, used to create
    markup languages such as DocBook.",
```

```
      "GlossSeeAlso": ["GML", "XML"]
                },
     "GlossSee": "markup"
         }
       }
     }
   }
 }
```

The JSON object structure requires you to create a temporary object in Delphi to parse JSON data. You have to create an intermediate object such as `TJSONObject`, `TJSONArray`, or `TJSONString`, to read or write JSON data.

We will address the return of the web service. To do this, follow these steps:

1. Modify the names for `edtName` and `edtEmail`.

2. Add a `System.JSON` unit at the `uses` interface:

    ```
    uses
        System.JSON;
    ```

3. Add some units at the `uses` implementation:

    ```
    uses
       REST.Utils, System.NetEncoding,
    Web.HTTPApp, System.Net.HttpClient, IdHTTP;
    ```

4. In the `public` area of the form, declare an `FAccessToken` variable as `String`:

    ```
    public
    {public declarations}
     FAccessToken : String;
    ```

5. Create a private function named `LoadPhoto` to load the profile photo of your user:

    ```
    function TForm1.LoadPhoto(url : string): TMemoryStream;
    var
            MS : TMemoryStream;
            photo: TBitmap;
            http : THTTPClient;
    begin
            MS := TMemoryStream.Create;
            http := THTTPClient.Create;

            photo := TBitmap.Create;
            try
    ```

```
                    try
                            http.Get(url, MS);

                    except on e: EIdHTTPProtocolException do
                    begin
                            if e.ErrorCode = 404 then
                            begin
                                    // url not found
                                    showmessage('Not found');
                            end
                            else
                            begin
                                    // error.
                                    showmessage('Error...');
                            end;
                    end;
                    end;

                    MS.Position := 0;
                    Result := MS;
            finally
                    photo.Free;
            end;
    end;
```

6. Create a private function named `extractString` to capture the JSON value as a string:

```
function TForm1.extractString(tNode: String; LJsonObj :
TJSONObject): String;
begin
  Try
    Result := StringReplace(
      TJSONObject(LJsonObj).Get(tNode).JsonValue.ToString,
        '"', '', [rfReplaceAll]);
  except
  end;
end;
```

7. Create a private procedure named `downloadPhoto` to download and show a profile photo:

```
procedure TForm1.downloadPhoto(url: string);
var
  MS : TMemoryStream;
begin
  // Download Photo
  Try
```

```
      MS := LoadPhoto(url);
      circle_photo.Fill.Bitmap.Bitmap.LoadFromStream(MS);
    Except
      Showmessage('Error');
    end;
  end;
```

8. In the `RESTRequest1` component, add code to the `AfterExecute` event:

```
procedure TForm1.RESTRequest1AfterExecute(Sender:
TCustomRESTRequest);
var
  LJsonObj : TJSONObject;
  LElements: TJSONValue;
  msg, url_photo, name, email, user_id : string;
begin
        try
                msg := '';
                FAccessToken := '';


                // Valid JSON
                if Assigned(RESTResponse1.JSONValue) then
                        msg := RESTResponse1.JSONValue.ToString;


                // Extract JSON fields
                LJsonObj := TJSONObject.ParseJSONValue(
                  TEncoding.UTF8.GetBytes(msg), 0) as TJSONObject;

                try
                        user_id :=
                          TNetEncoding.HTML.Decode(
                            StringReplace(TJSONObject(LJsonObj).
                             Get('id').JsonValue.ToString, '"',
'',
                               [rfReplaceAll]));
                except
                end;
                // email
                email := extractString('email', LJsonObj);
                // First Name
                name := extractString('first_name', LJsonObj);
                // Last Name
                name := name + ' ' + extractString('last_name',
LJsonObj);

                try
```

```
                    LElements :=
TJSONObject(TJSONObject(LJsonObj).
Get('picture').JsonValue).Get('data').JsonValue;

                    url_photo :=
StringReplace(TJSONObject(LElements).Get('url').
                    JsonValue.ToString.Replace('\','') ,
'"', '',

                    [rfReplaceAll]);
        except
        end;

        downloadPhoto(url_photo);

        edtName.Text := name;
        edtEmail.Text := email;


    except

    end;
end;
```

With the visual components on screen and partially configured, we added complexity by retrieving the JSON values from the Facebook fields. It is still premature to give an explanation because we have not finished the recipe, but it is worth mentioning that besides Facebook, any REST service that works with JSON objects will be considered.

By adding `System.JSON`, we are supporting our application for the JSON library, its objects, vectors, and so on.

We use the `TJSONObject` and `TJSONValue` classes to manipulate the JSON result received from the `RESTResponse` component. Every JSON object can have a vector, and within this vector, other objects, and within these objects, values.

The `TJSONValue` object represents a value and stands for a node in the XML template. For example, `email` is a JSON object that has a value. `TJSONValue` will represent the value in `string`, object, array, number, `bool`, `True`, `False`, and `null` values.

Next, we add the procedure that loads the photo from the Facebook URL and displays it inside the circle. Using a memory stream object, we are able to load an image by capturing it through its bytes and converting it to a bitmap. This process ensures that the loaded memory flow will be transferred to the circle component.

The `AfterExecute` event will be triggered after the completion of our login, loading the scope data.

Logging in with Facebook

You request an access token by opening the page. The access token is valid for only two hours. You can update the token in the background without the user having to log in again.

We have reached the last stage of this chapter. This is where we will add the final seasoning. To finally include the login functionality, you need to create a new form to receive a web page with which the user will interact to confirm their identity and to confirm the permissions requested by the application.

Coding login

Before encoding the login, we need to create a new form to display the Facebook authentication **Uniform Resource Identifier** (**URI**). By following the next steps alongside the new form, we will finally be able to complete our login:

1. Create a new form and name it `FormLogin`.
2. Set the **WindowState** property to **wsMaximized**.
3. Add a **TRectangle** and align it to the top.
4. Add a button inside the **TRectangle** component and align it to the left.
5. Add the **TWebBrowser** component and align **Client**. This component will be where the user validates the Facebook login.

   After adding the visual components and configuring them according to the preceding steps, save it. Your form should look like this:

 The **TWebBrowser** component has no color: at design time, it stays transparent. One tip, if you wish, is to modify the color of your form, so it gives the impression that the browser is colored.

6. Go back to the main form and add `FormLogin` to the `uses` clause:

```
uses
REST.Utils,
System.NetEncoding,Web.HTTPApp,System.Net.HttpClient,IdHTTP,
uFrmLogin;
```

7. Code the `ButtonClick` event of your login button:

```
procedure TForm1.btnLoginClick(Sender: TObject);
var
        app_id, LURL : string;
begin
        try
                FAccessToken := '';
                app_id := ''; // Your App ID here...

                LURL := 'https://www.facebook.com/dialog/oauth'
                        + '?client_id=' + URIEncode(app_id)
                        + '&response_type=token'
                        + '&scope=' +
URIEncode('public_profile,email')
                        + '&redirect_uri=' +
URIEncode('https://www.facebook.com/connect/login_success.html');


                // Open Facebook Login...
                try
                        FrmLogin := TFrmLogin.Create(nil);
                        FrmLogin.WebBrowser1.Navigate(LURL);
                        FrmLogin.ShowModal(
                           procedure(ModalResult: TModalResult)
                             begin
                               if FAccessToken <> '' then
                             begin
                               RESTRequest1.ResetToDefaults;
                               RESTClient1.ResetToDefaults;
                               RESTResponse1.ResetToDefaults;
RESTClient1.BaseURL:='https://graph.facebook.com';
                               RESTClient1.Authenticator :=
OAuth2Authenticator1;
                               RESTRequest1.Resource :=
'me?fields=first_name,
 last_name,email,
 picture.height(150)';

                               OAuth2Authenticator1.AccessToken :=
FAccessToken;

                               RESTRequest1.Execute;
```

```
                                         end;
                             end);
                  finally

                  end;
            except on e:exception do
                     showmessage(e.Message);
            end;
      end;
```

8. Copy the ID of your Facebook application and enter the source code from *step 5*. This ID will identify your application, its permissions, and so on, to Facebook.

9. Go back to `FormLogin` and create a new property in the `public` area:

```
public
property OnBeforeRedirect: TWebFormRedirectEvent read
FOnBeforeRedirect write FOnBeforeRedirect;
```

10. Note that the `TWebFormRedirectEvent` object is not declared. For this, we must add a `type` section:

```
type
   TWebFormRedirectEvent = procedure(const AURL : string; var
DoCloseWebView: boolean) of object;
```

11. Add `Unit1` to the `uses` clause:

```
implementation

{$R *.fmx}

uses
   Unit1;
```

12. Create a new procedure in `FormLogin` named `Facebook_AccessTokenRedirect`:

```
procedure Facebook_AccessTokenRedirect(const AURL: string; var
DoCloseWebView: boolean);
var
      LATPos: integer;
      LToken: string;
begin
      try
             LATPos := Pos('access_token=', AURL);

             if (LATPos > 0) then
```

```
                        begin
                            LToken := Copy(AURL, LATPos + 13,
        Length(AURL));

                            if (Pos('&', LToken) > 0) then
                            begin
                                    LToken := Copy(LToken, 1, Pos('&',
        LToken) - 1);
                            end;

                            Form1.FAccessToken := LToken;

                            if (LToken <> '') then
                            begin
                                    DoCloseWebView := True;
                            end;
                        end
                        else
                        begin

                            LATPos := Pos('api_key=', AURL);

                            if LATPos <= 0 then
                            begin
                                    LATPos := Pos('access_denied',
        AURL);

                                    if (LATPos > 0) then
                                    begin
                                        // Denied, Not Allow
                                        Form1.FAccessToken := '';
                                        DoCloseWebView := True;
                                    end;
                            end;
                        end;
                except
                    on E: Exception do
                        ShowMessage(E.Message);
                END;
            end;
```

13. Add code to `DidFinishLoad` in the `WebBrowser` event:

```
procedure TFrmLogin.WebBrowser1DidFinishLoad(ASender: TObject);
var
        CloseWebView : boolean;
        url : string;
begin
        url := TWebBrowser(ASender).URL;
```

```
            CloseWebView := false;

            if url <> '' then
                    Facebook_AccessTokenRedirect(url, CloseWebView);

            if CloseWebView then
            begin
                    TWebBrowser(ASender).Stop;
                    TWebBrowser(ASender).URL := '';
                    FrmLogin.close;
                    ModalResult := mrok;
            end;
    end;
```

This is how the form looks:

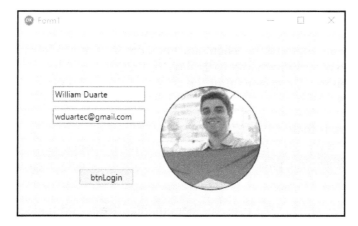

After performing some small refactoring and adding new features to `FormLogin`, you can request the access token by opening a web page for a Facebook page URL. The base URL is `https://www.facebook.com/dialog/oauth`.

Behind the scenes

This chapter does not specifically use the Facebook SDK; we need to send the parameters for connections in the default login flow for the web.

This variable that will be sent in the URL is the customer ID, the one you received after registering your application:

```
client_id = {CLIENTID}
```

Now let's use the `uri` constant provided by Facebook. Without this `uri` constant, you will not be able to validate the login:

```
redirect_uri = https: //www.facebook.com/connect/login_success.html
```

We need to use the token with the value for `response_type`. The access token is valid for two hours; when necessary, revalidate. The primary purpose of login is to get this access token:

```
response_type = token
```

The `scope` parameter contains the list of permissions to acquire. Facebook has recently changed the policy for obtaining permissions from its users through applications. By default, the only permissions available at the time of creating your application on the platform are **Profile** and **Email**:

```
scope = {target scopes}
```

That said, when we set up the REST client and the authenticator to fetch Facebook's base URL and direct it to comply with login, display, and redirect to the successful page, the API will return the token to us, and only after the token is returned will we seek the information allowed in the scope.

When the login page is loaded, your application will fire the `WebBrowser1DidFinishLoad` event. In this event, the page will be read in order to fetch the access token. Once in possession of this object, the page can be closed, and then the cursor redirects the original modal call.

When we request the name of the user, his/her email address, and his/her profile picture, respectively, in the `RESTRequest1.Resource: = 'me? Fields = first_name, last_name, email, picture.height (150)'` line, we are telling the request component that the resource is a name, email, and photo. We insert the access token, which has already been captured and saved in the `FAccessToken` variable.

And voila! When executing the REST call, we have a JSON object ready, containing all this information.

A JSON response can be transformed into any `TDataSet` descendant class. Data should be in a standard format for primitive data, such as `int`, `string`, `float`, and `bool`.

Only one component is required for this—the **TRESTDataSetAdapter**. Its usability is combined with **TClientDataSet**, so it is possible to immediately convert a JSON object into a dataset.

Summary

In this chapter, we learned interesting concepts about REST APIs, authentication, security, and, of course, how to log in to one of the most popular social networks, Facebook.

The first step was to create a direct application on the Facebook platform, selecting the desired login type (login flow for web) and some other additional information, such as application name, permissions, and application ID, among others.

With the application ID in hand, we started building our Delphi application to interact using the REST component suite with Facebook.

It is noteworthy that, without the correct configuration of the components and following the technical standards of connection of the platform, none of this would be possible. The same goes for any REST API service that's available. Some will use OAuth2, like Facebook; others will not. What's important to note is the level of security and how secure your application will be for external connections.

By getting a token for access, we can finally, with a user's permission, log in to your profile and get your personal data, including your profile picture.

In our next chapter, the project will be a hybrid application, where we will learn how to develop applications that will perform as services on different platforms: Windows services, Android services, and iOS background.

Further reading

For more information about Facebook login types, including access permissions, go to `https://developers.facebook.com/docs/facebook-login/manually-build-a-login-flow` and `https://developers.facebook.com/docs/facebook-login/permissions`.

3
Cross-Platform Services for Windows, iOS, and Android

Service applications work by receiving requests from client applications. They then process these by returning data to the users. Usually, these run in the background with little or no human interference. Web internet services, the **File Transfer Protocol** (**FTP**), and email servers are examples of service applications.

A service or application service is required to perform tasks behind the scenes. Certain types of tasks do not necessarily need interaction with the screen or the **graphical user interface** (**GUI**). An alarm clock is one example of this type of service; while a previous configuration is required to inform the computer of the alarm time, it is not necessary to keep the application open—you can just set it up and the alarm will be triggered at the right time.

Another example of an application service is the internet; for instance, when using a URL address, a request is sent to an HTTP server that, as a service, will respond with the content of the page.

In this chapter, we will make three application services on different platforms—each with their own particularities.

The application services will not interact with each other. They will be independent services showing the characteristics of what can be developed in Windows, Android, and iOS.

Windows services, also known as **NT services**, provide long-running executable applications that run in their own Windows sessions. The services can initiate themselves as soon as the computer boots. Additionally, they can be restarted, paused, and even blocked from being viewed by any user.

Android service is an application without a graphical interface that performs tasks in the background. There are only two types of services—started and bound. An app can also contain multiple services.

iOS' **UIBackgroundModes** works by assigning an application to enable specific background services. For example, applications can use the change location interface to receive location events instead of registering as a background application location.

The knowledge that is needed to understand this chapter is intermediate.

In this chapter, we will introduce you to the concepts and construction of services on three platforms that are supported by Delphi:

- Building Windows services
- Building Android services
- iOS background mode

Technical requirements

To get started, you must have a version of Delphi installed on your computer. For example, we'll use Delphi Rio, but you can use your version of Delphi as long as it's from Delphi 10 Seattle or a later version. You also need to run a physical Android device or emulator. If you want to test in an Apple environment, you will need a Mac with macOS and an iOS device or simulator. Previous experience of compiling on iOS is also required as it is not covered in this chapter.

The code files for this chapter are present on GitHub at `https://github.com/ PacktPublishing/Delphi-Programming-Projects/tree/master/Chapter03`.

Project overview

In this chapter, we'll cover the creation of services for Windows, Android, and iOS background mode.

The estimated build time is 5 minutes for Windows, 10 minutes for Android, and 5 minutes for iOS.

Getting started

You must have a Mac device with macOS in order to compile iOS. A Windows computer is enough to compile Windows and Android services.

Creating Windows services

If you are looking to create an application that is always available online and requires little or no human intervention, then a Windows service is the option to go for. By creating a Windows service, we can delegate the responsibility of starting the application for Windows itself, among other advantages.

Delphi already has a base project in its wizard, which is readily available for creating a Windows service; just go to **File** | **New** | **Other** | **Delphi** | **Windows** | **Windows Service**:

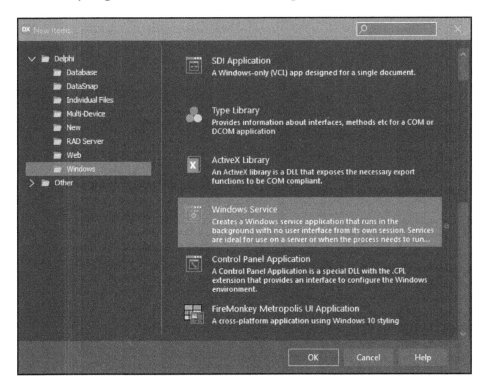

In newer versions of Delphi, the visual framework—either **Visual Component Library** (**VCL**) or FMX—is decoupled. That is, projects don't necessarily come with one of these frameworks installed by default. If, in your IDE, you receive the message to include the VCL, then confirm it as follows:

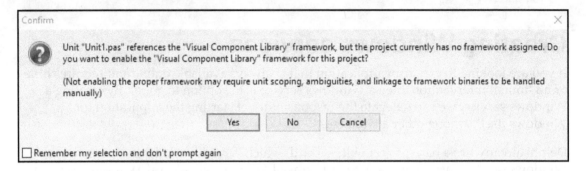

Delphi, as mentioned earlier, will create a new project with a unit containing the service class (which is a descendant of the `TService` class) along with two implemented methods: `ServiceController` and `GetServiceController`. These methods are necessary for the execution of the service, hence no changes have to be made to these functions.

In Windows services, we essentially have a default application built by the Delphi IDE wizard, where the `TService` class is implemented as a `DataModule` container.

This created unit contains a type of `DataModule` form; it contains events and properties that are crucial to the operation of the service. Let's take a look at some of the main events of service execution:

- **OnStart**: This event runs as soon as the service is started.

- **OnExecute**: This is the event where the functionality of the service will be implemented; it is executed soon after the **OnStart** event, that is, when the service goes live—it works in a similar way to thread execution.

- **OnStop**: This event runs as soon as the service is stopped.

- **OnPause**: This event runs when the service is paused.

- **OnContinue**: This event is executed when the service restarts after a pause.

In addition to the execution events, there are also service installation events:

- **BeforeInstall/AfterInstall**: These events are executed before or after the service installation.

There are essential properties for the proper functioning of a Windows service, including the following:

- **StartType**: This property sets the startup mode of the service. By default, this option is marked as **stAuto**, which means that the service will start alongside Windows. In addition to the **stAuto** option, there is the **stManual** option, which means that the service must be started manually; and the **stDisabled** option, which means that only an administrator can start the service.

- **DisplayName**: This property defines the name that will be displayed for the service in the Windows Services Manager.

- **Dependencies**: This property defines a list of dependencies for the execution of the service; that is, the service will only start if all of its dependencies (which are other services) are started.

- **Interactive**: This property states whether the communication between the service and desktop is feasible or not (for example, with `ShowMessage`). This is subject to the type of service that is being created.

Now that you know some basic properties and events of the `TService` object, let's build a service that will be responsible for writing a message in a text file every 10 seconds.

Make sure that you are in a form that is a `DataModule` form, as follows:

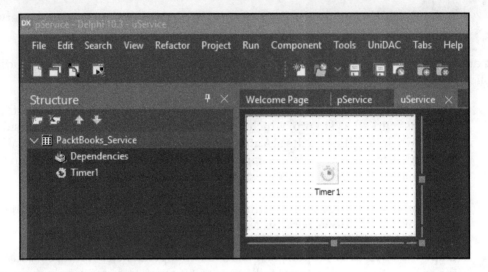

Now perform the following steps:

1. Add a **Timer1** component to the form.

2. Set **Interval** to `10000` milliseconds (or 10 seconds).

3. Set **Enabled** to `False`.

4. Change the **Name** property of `Service1` to `PacktBooks_Service`.

5. Double-click on the **OnExecute** event and enter the following code:

```
procedure TPacktBooks_Service.ServiceExecute(Sender: TService);
begin
  Timer1.Enabled := True;
  while not Terminated do
    ServiceThread.ProcessRequests(True);
  Timer1.Enabled := False;
end;
```

What this code does, in the **OnExecute** event, is start a thread that enables or disables the timer.

6. Then, we set the **Timer1** component. To do this, click on the **Timer1** component, go to the event tab, and then double-click on the **Timer1** component, and add the following code:

```
procedure TPacktBooks_Service.Timer1Timer(Sender: TObject);
Const
  FileName = 'c:\temp\Chapter3_WindowsServices.txt';
var
  F: TextFile;
begin
  AssignFile(f,FileName);

  if FileExists(FileName) then
    Append(f)
  else
    Rewrite(f);

  writeln(f,DateTimeToStr(Now));
  CloseFile(f);
end;
```

Here, we are using the basics of reading and writing files. With the `TextFile` class, we control the text file by writing the current date to each iteration of the **Timer1** component. We set the directory to save the text file, such as the `C:\temp` root and the name of our `Chapter3_WindowsServices.txt` file. This seems enough, minimally, to have a service in operation.

If all is correct, proceed by saving your project, naming the main unit as `uService.pas`, and the project as `pService.dproj`. Then, build it using *Shift + F9*.

Installing and uninstalling a service

Now we have an executable file, which is ready to write to a text file. All that remains is to install this service, so that it can be executed, and then proceed with what it was programmed for.

Service Control Manager (**SCM**) is the service that is used for installing other Windows services. There are two ways in which you can view the installed services:

- **Task Manager**
- The **Services** panel:

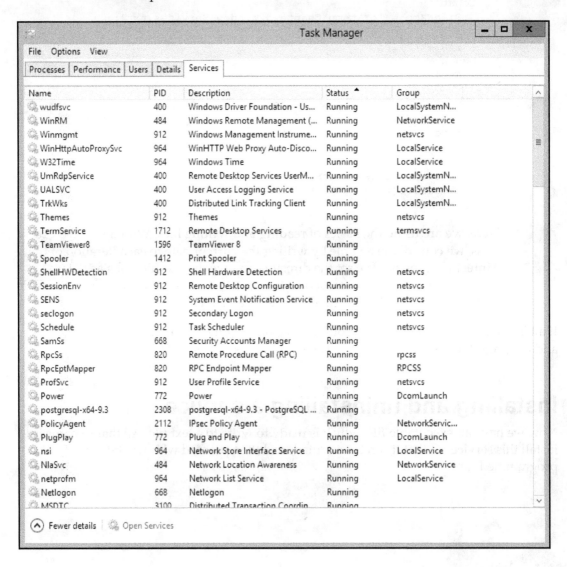

In the preceding screenshot, we have the **Services** tab in the Windows **Task Manager**. The other way to view the services is to start, stop, restart, and view their dependencies through the Windows + *R* shortcut and enter `services.msc` in the **Run** window, and then hit **Run**. The following screen should appear:

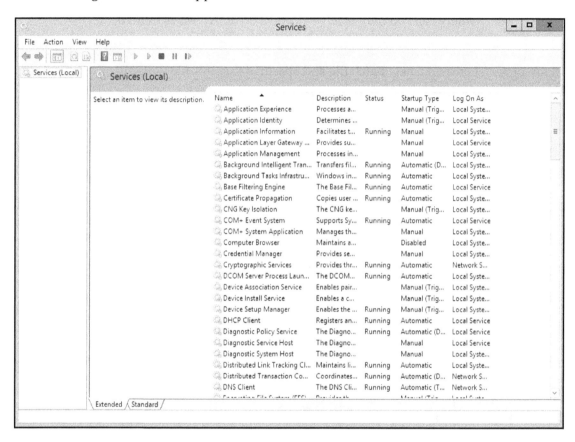

So, now you know where the Windows Service Manager is, and you know that you can **Start**, **Stop**, **Pause**, and **Restart** any Windows service.

In order to install the service, click on **Start** and select **Run**, and then type `"YourPath\pService.exe" /INSTALL`. Then, click on **OK**.

A Windows service needs to be installed and then run. There are a number of ways in which you can install a service. The simplest and most practical way is to use batch commands; that is, the `/INSTALL` and `/UNINSTALL` commands.

An alternative is to create a batch file and run it in the folder of your main service executable.

> In order for the batch file to work, you must specify the full path of the executable file, no matter where you are, and run it as an administrator. Otherwise, you may receive a code 5 error: **Access is denied**.

In my project, I created a new batch file and specified that this file will call the /INSTALL parameter:

After installing the service, we can check whether it will be automatic, manual, or disabled. The automatic mode is when the service starts automatically with Windows, that is, during restart. However, to start manually, we can use the net command in standard Windows.

> On successfully installing the service, a confirmation dialog box pops up. Otherwise, an error message pops up. The installation may fail due to the absence of the required rights. To avoid viewing the confirmation dialog box, add the /silent switch as pService.exe /install /silent.

After installing the service, we can view the service in the **Services** management panel:

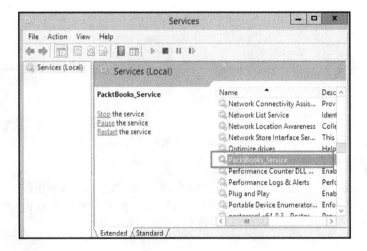

To uninstall the service, you need to proceed with the /UNINSTALL command. You can use the same methods mentioned previously for the installation—either through the **Start** menu or by using a batch file.

For example, an Uninstall.bat file will use the following command:

```
"C:\FullPath\pService.exe" /UNINSTALL /SILENT
```

If you return to the Windows Service Manager, you will notice that it is no longer in the list of installed services.

When uninstalling a service that is running, it will be **marked for deletion** and will remain enabled until the user stops it. In this case, the service will be deleted automatically after being stopped.

Starting and stopping

When you install certain types of programs, you may need to restart services in order to avoid conflicts. Regardless of why you need to control services, you need to understand when to start and stop them.

The traditional method is in the **Services** panel by services.msc or by **Task Manager**. Select the **Installed Service** option and right-click and select the service to start it. Or, simply, under the name of the service in the panel itself, click on the **Start** hotlink:

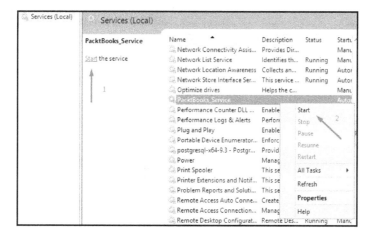

When we start or run the service, we are invoking the **OnExecute** event (which we already programmed in *step 5* at the beginning of this chapter). This will then trigger the event that will execute our code to create the text file, incrementing the current date and time every 10 seconds:

```
procedure TPacktBooks_Service.ServiceExecute(Sender: TService);
begin
  Timer1.Enabled := True;
  while not Terminated do
    ServiceThread.ProcessRequests(True);
  Timer1.Enabled := False;
end;
```

There are several ways to start or stop a service; one method is to use the Windows NET.exe executable through Command Prompt (DOS). This mode works with any service—provided that you have its name. This technique can also be extended to a batch file:

```
net start PacktBooks_Service
```

After executing the commands, the service will be started, as follows:

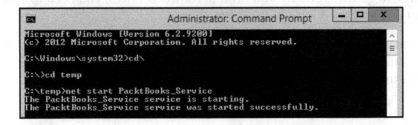

 Note that in this case, it is not necessary to enter the full path or directory of the service. You simply need the name of the service, which also can't be confused with the name of the executable.

The service, if properly installed and executed, should have recorded some dates and times in our file. Remember that we selected the **Timer1** component so that it will trigger the recording of the current date and time in a file, called Chapter3_WindowsServices.txt, every 10 seconds.

Check the file in your directory and see everything happen without any iteration from the end user—yes, this is a running service.

Now, if we want to stop the service, we will use the `stop` command on our Command Prompt:

```
net stop PacktBooks_Service
```

It is also possible to start and stop a service using the Delphi code; some programmers choose to build a **Control Panel** type of application, which will run inside Windows' **Control Panel**—Firebird Guardian is an example of this.

Debugging a service

As we already know, the application service has no interaction with the end user. Additionally, it has no visual interface (GUI), so there is no way to control whether a certain button is clicked on or whether a form is opened, because, in this case, they do not exist.

One way to run the in-service **Debug** mode is through the Delphi **Attach to Process** menu.

 In Windows 10, if Delphi is not running as an administrator, some processes may not be shown (even if the service that created it has been registered as an administrator). To avoid this kind of problem, run the Delphi IDE as an administrator.

To test this, perform the following steps:

1. Enter a breakpoint in the desired line of code.
2. Make sure that the service is currently running.
3. In Delphi, under **Run | Attach to Process**, and select the **PID** process corresponding to the running service.

4. Debug it as follows:

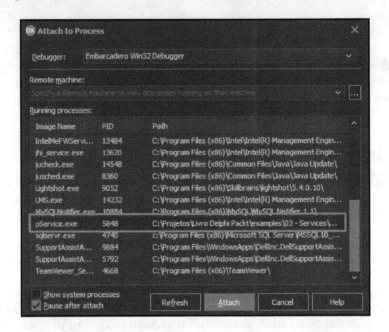

If you see the **CPU** tab in your debug screen, it means that the code being debugged is not the exact code that is compiled. To do this, perform **Build All** and try again.

Debugging a service is not a difficult task, but it is unconventional. We have seen that it is enough to use the **Attach To Process** feature, since the service is already running, and to then debug it.

Service threads

Every service has its own thread; it's important to make sure that the implementation of your services is secure, especially if your application service implements more than one service. The purpose of building `TServiceThread` is to implement the service in the `TService` thread's **OnExecute** event handler. The service thread has an `Execute` method, which consists of a loop that calls the **OnStart** and **OnExecute** events of the service before dealing with new requests.

The processing time for a particular service request can be high, and the service can receive more than one request from multiple clients. Hence, generating a fresh thread for each request and shifting the request from that service implementation to the `Execute` method of the fresh thread is an efficient way to deal with such an instance.

This means that you will not schedule the **OnExecute** event of your service, but the **OnStart** events, which starts the service by creating the new thread. When you stop and continue running a service by using the Windows **Services** panel, the suspend and resume actions will be triggered on your **TThread**:

1. In the interface section of your unit, declare a new `TThread` descendant named `TNewServiceThread` (`TServiceThread` already exists). This is the thread that does the job for your service:

```
TNewServiceThread = class(TThread)
   public
      procedure Execute; override;
   end;
```

2. Create a new type variable, called `ServiceThread`, in the global scope of our service:

```
var
  NewServiceThread : TNewServiceTherad;
```

3. Replicate a code that is similar to the `Timer` event in the `Execute` event of the new thread:

```
procedure TNewServiceThread.Execute;
const
  FileName = 'c:\Chapter3_WindowsServices_SafeThread.txt'; //new
filename
var
  F: TextFile;
begin
  while not Terminated do
   begin
     AssignFile(f,FileName);

      if FileExists(FileName) then
        Append(f)
      else
        Rewrite(f);

     writeln(f,DateTimeToStr(Now));
     CloseFile(f);
```

```
        Sleep(10000); //simulate timer
    end;
end;
```

4. In the **OnStart** event, add the following code:

```
procedure TPacktBooks_Service.ServiceStart(Sender: TService;
    var Started: Boolean);
begin
    NewServiceThread := TNewServiceThread.Create(False);
    Started := True;
end;
```

5. In the **OnContinue** event, add the following code:

```
procedure TPacktBooks_Service.ServiceContinue(Sender: TService;
    var Continued: Boolean);
begin
    NewServiceThread.Resume;
    Continued := True;
end;
```

6. In the **OnPause** event, add the following code:

```
procedure TPacktBooks_Service.ServicePause(Sender: TService;
    var Paused: Boolean);
begin
    NewServiceThread.Suspend;
    Paused := True;
end;
```

7. Then, in the **OnStop** event, add the following code:

```
procedure TPacktBooks_Service.ServiceStop(Sender: TService;
    var Stopped: Boolean);
begin
    NewServiceThread.Terminate;
    Stopped := True;
end;
```

With this, you have control of the execution of the thread of your service and can manage practically all the events.

Creating Android services

An Android service is a non-UI application that performs tasks in the background.

There are essentially two types of service:

- **Start service**: This service is started by an Android application. The service may run in the background indefinitely, even if the application is closed.

- **Bind service**: This service only works while it is connected to an Android application. More than one application can connect to the same service.

Let's create an **Android Service** by performing the following steps:

1. Create a new Delphi project by going to **File | New| Delphi**. Notice that we have the **Android Service** option, as follows:

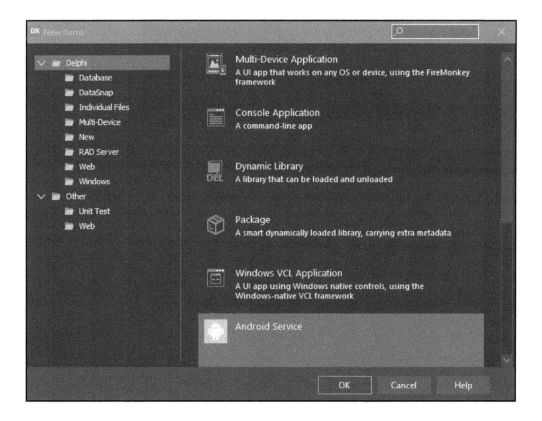

2. Select this option. Then, we need to define the service option that we want to create; in our case, we will choose **Local Service**:

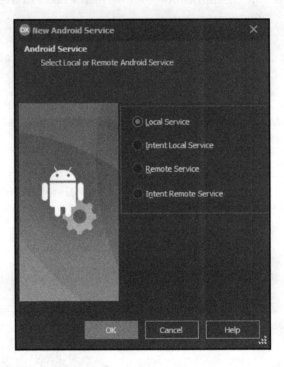

3. After this process, the project will be loaded into the IDE; in **Project Manager** (*Ctrl + Alt + F11*) rename our project to `PacktAndroidService`.

4. Rename `Unit1` as `uPacktAndroidServiceDM`. In `uPacktAndroidServiceDM`, we will add in the `uses` section of the implementation using the following line of code:

```
uses Androidapi.JNI.App;
```

5. Click on save and let's take a look at the start service.

Start services

Essentially, there are two types of start services:

- START_STICKY is used for services that are explicitly started and stopped as needed.
- START_NOT_STICKY is used for services that should only remain running while processing all the commands that are sent to them.

Let's start START_STICKY. Our service will start and it will remain running even if the application is closed; to do this, we will perform the following steps:

1. Encode the main **OnStartCommand** event as follows:

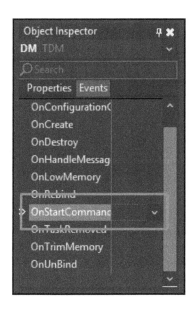

Here, simply add one line of code:

```
function TDM.AndroidServiceStartCommand(const Sender: TObject;
  const Intent: JIntent; Flags, StartId: Integer): Integer;
begin
  Result := TJService.JavaClass.START_STICKY;
end;
```

2. To demonstrate that our application service is up and running, we'll add an onscreen notification component—**TNotificationCenter**.

3. Add the `System.DateUtil` and `System.Threading` interfaces to the `uses` section:

```
System.Threading, System.DateUtils
```

5. In the `public` declarations, include a `T : ITask` variable, as follows:

```
public
    { Public declarations }
    T : ITask;
end;
```

6. In the `public` declarations, include a procedure, as follows:

```
public
    { Public declarations }
    T : ITask;
    procedure LaunchNotification(Name, Title, Body : String);
end;
```

7. Now let's program the notification procedure, as follows:

```
procedure TDM.LaunchNotification(Name, Title, Body: String);
var
  Notify : TNotification;
begin
  Notify := NotificationCenter1.CreateNotification;
  Try
    Notify.Name  := Name;
    Notify.Title := Title;
    Notify.AlertBody := Body;
    Notify.FireDate := IncSecond(Now,1);
    NotificationCenter1.ScheduleNotification(Notify);
  Finally
    Notify.Free;
  End;
end;
```

8. It is necessary to return to the main **OnStartCommand** event to now include the procedure call that will trigger the notification:

```
function TDM.AndroidServiceStartCommand(const Sender: TObject;
  const Intent: JIntent; Flags, StartId: Integer): Integer;
begin
  Result := TJService.JavaClass.START_STICKY;
  T := TTask.Run( procedure
   begin
    while True do
      sleep(10);
      LaunchNotification('Packt Delphi Book', 'Delphi Rocks',
        'This is Chapter 3!');
      exit;
   end
  )
end;
```

Our application service is complete, and we now need to move to the host application. To finish, save the project and make a build.

Host applications

So, now we need to create an application that will host this service.

In the same project that is open, we can create new projects by keeping them in a project group. To keep services organized, we will keep the same rule for the example of this chapter, which is to create a project group. To do this, perform the following steps:

1. In **Project Manager**, select the **Add New Project** option and then select **New | Multi-Device Application**. Then, select **Blank Application**.

2. While still in **Project Manager**, rename the second project to PacktHostApp and its unit to uFrmHostService.

3. Select **File** | **Save All** (*Shift* + *Ctrl* + *S*) and name the project group `PacktGroupAndroidServices`:

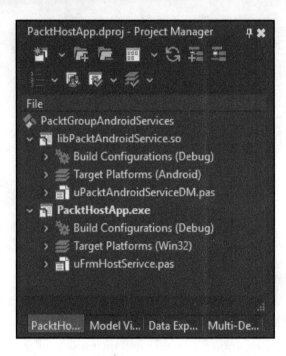

4. In the `uses` section of the `uFrmHostService` unit section, declare the following namespace after the existing ones:

```
System.Android.Service
```

5. In the `private` section of the form, we will add a connection to the local service:

```
private
  { Private declarations }
  ConnService : TLocalServiceConnection;
```

6. Create a new button and insert the form, and enter the following text to start the service:

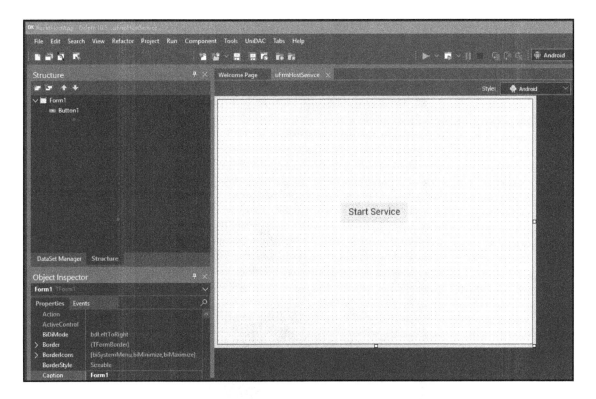

7. Then, code it as follows:

```
procedure TForm1.Button1Click(Sender: TObject);
begin
  ConnService := TLocalServiceConnection.Create;
  ConnService.StartService('PacktAndroidService');
end;
```

 Note the `PacktAndroidService` service name. This name will be generated based on the project name and the file generated by your service.

It's not over yet; it's necessary to bind the service inside the client application, after all, it is a local service. Remember to save everything.

Adding an Android service to the host

Now we will make a build in the `libPacktAndroidService.so` project and make it available to our application by performing the following steps:

1. In **Project Manager** select the `PacktHostApp` project, right-click on the **Android SDK**, and then select the **Add Android Service...** option:

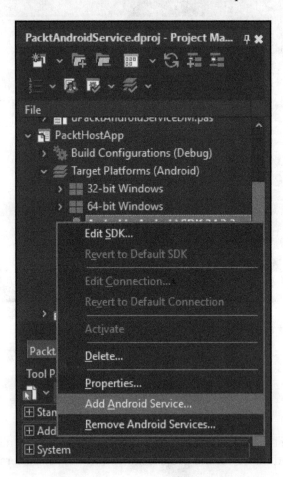

2. Select the first **Search Files...** option.

3. Select the directory where the `libPacktAndroidService.so` project is saved:

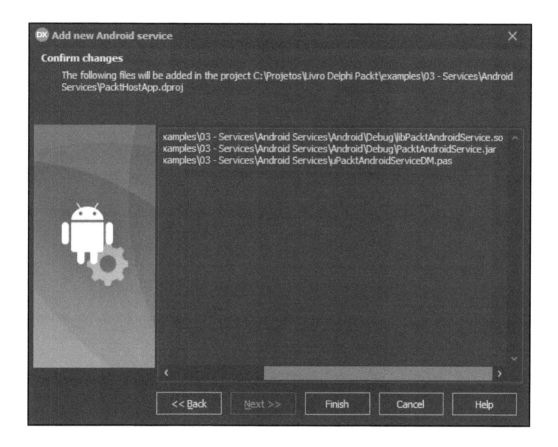

Note that a new `.jar` file is now in the additional libraries of the host application:

The problem with this approach is that the service stays by depending on the application being open and being started.

Local services or remote services

Unlike Windows, on Android you can work with two types of services, both remote and local. In short, a local service runs in the same process as the client application, in the case of a remote service, the process may be in another application. Let's have a look at the **Local Service** and **Remote Service** options in Android:

- **Local Service**: You can use this option to create a local service. An Android application interacts directly with the service and is running in the same process. This option uses the following line of code in the `\Android\Debug\AndroidManifest.xml` file:

```
<service android:exported="false"
android:name="com.embarcadero.services<service_name>" />
```

- **Remote Service**: You can use this option to create a remote service. Selecting this option includes the following line of code in the `\Android\Debug\AndroidManifest.xml` file of the Android application, which is linked to the Android service:

```
<service android:exported="true"
android:name="com.embarcadero.services.<service_name>" />
```

iOS background mode

Forget the concept of Windows services and Android services; in iOS, things are a bit different. You need to make few modifications if you want your application to perform a task while running in the background on iOS, since this functionality is not offered by default in Delphi for iOS.

A file named `<appname>.info.plist` is created when Delphi compiles your iOS application to the selected release type (**Debug** or **Release**). In `<appname>.info.plist`, `<appname>` is your application name and this file is deployed to iOS as `info.plist`. This is the file that iOS uses to determine whether your application uses background services.

Background services supported on iOS are described in detail in the Apple iOS documentation at `http://embt.co/UIBackgroundModes`.

All in info.plist

To support background processing for any or all of these services, you need to edit and copy the `<appname>.info.plist` file manually. This is because Delphi overwrites the original file every time you compile.

After you've copied the `<appname>` `.info.plist` file, you can edit the file with an editor such as Notepad++ or Sublime Text. Then, anywhere inside the `<dict>` tag, add the following code:

```
<key>UIBackgroundModes</key>
 <array>
   <string>location</string>
 </array>
```

This seems to be a rather bureaucratic way, doesn't it?

An alternative, if you are using a previous version of Delphi Rio, is to perform the following steps:

1. Navigate to **Project Options | Version Info**.

2. Right-click on the list views of **Key** and **Value and** select the **Add Key** option.

3. Then, add **UIBackgroundModes Key**, as follows:

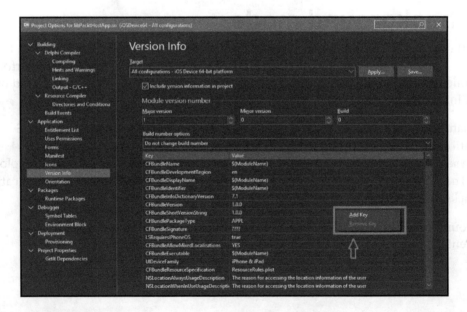

In this way, you give the application permission to perform certain tasks in the background (according to the scope), or better, according to the background mode:

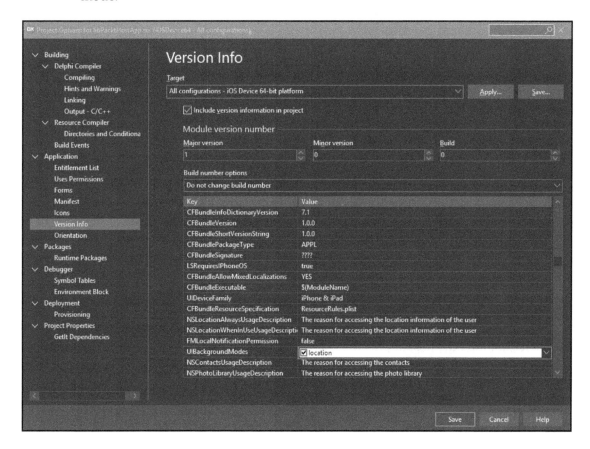

In the preceding screenshot, the **UIBackgroundModes** location has been added.

All interaction takes place through the `.plist` file. You can change it manually, but it is easier and safer to change these settings through the **Version Info** option in the project menu.

Summary

In this chapter, we initially learned about the concept of a service and how each platform can support a service. We split the chapter into three parts: Windows, Android, and iOS—one part for each platform.

When working with Windows services, we learned that a service is an application that runs without user interference and has no graphical interface. So, we built a service where, every 10 seconds, we recorded the current date and time into a text file.

Additionally, we learned that the **OnExecute** event forms the backbone of a service with its looping or main thread. However, when we receive many requests or require a multithread service instead, we opt to manually handle the execution and stop the events using safe threads.

Next, we gained an understanding about Android services. This also performs tasks in the background, but it is at least necessary to have a host application. We learned that Delphi provides full support to the available service types, but we focused primarily on `START_STICKY`.

In our service application, we used some new units—this was simply to manipulate the Delphi and Android threads and services API, as it was necessary to display a message or alert the user using local notifications.

We then examined the host application—essentially, we found that it requires knowing whether you are using a local service or remote service, and the name of the service. To use the service on the host, you also need to link your `.jar` library.

Finally, we covered iOS background modes. These are not proper services and Apple calls them **UIBackgroundModes**.

We learned that the operation allows certain functionality to continue running in the background, such as audio activities, locations, and more.

In the next chapter, we will create a database, explore Delphi interfaces, and do the testing for our application.

Further reading

For more information, you can refer to the following links:

- **Windows services**: http://docwiki.embarcadero.com/RADStudio/Tokyo/en/Service_Applications

- **Android services**: http://docwiki.embarcadero.com/RADStudio/Tokyo/en/Creating_Android_Services

- **iOS background mode**: https://developer.apple.com/library/archive/documentation/General/Reference/InfoPlistKeyReference/Articles/iPhoneOSKeys.html#//apple_ref/doc/uid/TP40009252-SW22

4
Design Patterns to Build a Multi-Database System

Design patterns are structures and relationships that we use repeatedly in object-oriented projects. Understanding them can help you to design better (and thereby improve the development of your software) and design systems that are more complex.

The application of design patterns can improve the quality of the systems that are developed, because they are, in practice, tested and approved solutions to common problems within the programming.

With the use of standards, you can reduce coupling, improve the readability of your code, and increase the degree of reuse of the code. Standards also help other developers to understand your code more quickly.

According to the book *Design Patterns: Reusable Object-Oriented Software Solutions*, by John Vlissides, Ralph Johnson, Richard Helm, and Erich Gamma (the **Gang of Four** (**GoF**)), design patterns are divided into 23 types. Due to this large number of standards, it was necessary to classify them according to their purposes.

According to the GoF, design patterns are divided into three categories:

- Creational
- Structural
- Behavioral

Delphi fully implements an object-oriented language with a lot of refinements that simplify development.

The attribute classes of a particular pattern, which are also the most important, are the basic inheritance classes; abstract and virtual methods; and the use of the `protected` and `public` scope. They provide tools for creating patterns that can be reused and extended, and allow you to isolate varied database functionality from immutable attributes.

In this chapter, our goal will be to develop a multi-database system using some design patterns. Basically, we will use a few patterns. The secret of learning and using certain patterns is that we do not have to use all, or several, in a system. Moderate usage does well, and of course, the code becomes more readable and maintainable.

You will need an intermediate level of knowledge to understand this chapter.

The following topics will be covered in this chapter:

- Creating a database
- Models for databases – objects
- Exploring Delphi interfaces
- Repositories
- Presentation and final testing

Technical requirements

To get started, you must have a version of Delphi installed on your computer. For our examples, we'll use Delphi Rio, but you can use your version of Delphi, as long as it's from Seattle 10 or later.

The code files for this chapter are present on GitHub, at `https://github.com/PacktPublishing/Delphi-Programming-Projects/tree/master/Chapter04`.

Project overview

In this chapter, we will build a system that will connect and use two different database managers, using some design patterns for development.

The estimated build time is five minutes.

Getting started

For the multi-database solution, we will use the SQL Server Express and PostgreSQL databases. Any version is supported. In this chapter, the SQL Server 2008 R2 Express Edition will be used (a higher version can be used without problems), and so will PostgreSQL 9.3 (higher versions are also supported).

Creating a database

Before we start to code in Delphi, it is necessary to have the databases created, and to then connect to those databases in Delphi.

For our project in this chapter, we will work with three tables:

- users
- products
- customers

If you have not installed SQL Server 2008 R2 Express Edition (free) or PostgreSQL 9.3 (also free), you can use the database of your choice, but for the best use of this chapter, we strongly recommend that you follow the instructions contained herein:

- **To download SQL Server**: https://www.microsoft.com/en-us/sql-server/sql-server-editions-express
- **To download PostgreSQL**: https://www.enterprisedb.com/downloads/postgres-postgresql-downloads

The installation and configuration of the SQL Server and PostgreSQL database managers will not be covered in this chapter.

Creating an SQL Server database

To create the database and its tables in SQL Server, we will connect to our server through the database management system:

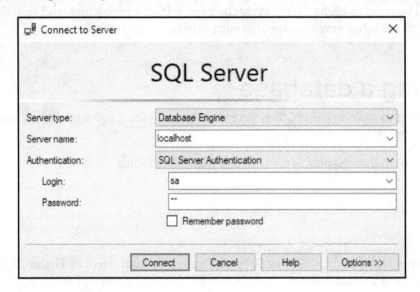

In the preceding screenshot, I am using SQL Server 2008 R2; however, you can use a higher version. The SQL version is not relevant in this case.

Next, we will create the database (the database file itself). There are two ways: one uses the form panel visually, and the other uses SQL code.

As a more didactic and illustrative example, we will visually create the database with the following steps:

1. With the server connected, select the **Database** tab and right-click on **New Database...**:

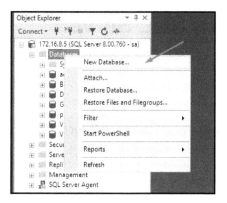

2. Give the database the name PACKT, and confirm:

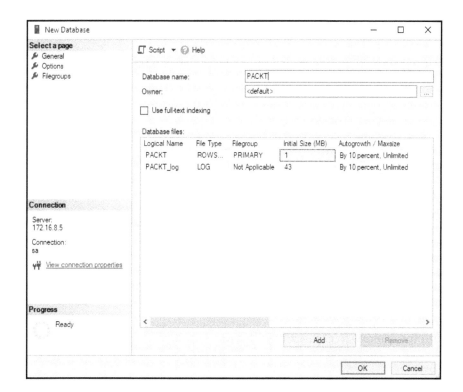

Once this is done, the PACKT database will be created on your disk drive.

Creating tables in SQL Server

Once you have created the PACKT database, you can create the users, products, and customers tables.

To do this, follow these steps:

1. With the PACKT database selected in **Object Explorer**, create a new query.
2. Write the SQL code for the creation of the following tables:

   - The SQL code for the users table is as follows:

     ```
     CREATE TABLE users(
      id_user int IDENTITY(1,1) NOT NULL PRIMARY KEY,
       login varchar(50) NOT NULL,
       password varchar(50) NOT NULL
       )
     ```

   - The SQL code for the products table is as follows:

     ```
     CREATE TABLE products (
       id_product int IDENTITY(1,1) NOT NULL PRIMARY KEY,
       code varchar(15),
       descr varchar(100),
       list_price float,
       tax float,
       quantity float
       )
     ```

   - The SQL code for the customers table is as follows:

     ```
     CREATE TABLE customers (
       id_customer int IDENTITY(1,1) NOT NULL PRIMARY KEY,
       customer_name varchar(150),
       customer_status int
       )
     ```

3. Run the queries to create the tables individually:

```
Microsoft SQL Server Management Studio
Debug   Tools   Window   Help
New Query
Execute  Debug
SQLQuery1.sql - 172....BDReport (sa (56))*
        CREATE TABLE users(
        id_user int IDENTITY(1,1) NOT NULL PRIMARY KEY,
         login varchar(50) NOT NULL,
         password varchar(50) NOT NULL
         )

         CREATE TABLE products (
        id_product int IDENTITY(1,1) NOT NULL PRIMARY KEY,
        code varchar(15),
        descr varchar(100),
        list_price float,
        tax float,
        quantity float
         )

        CREATE TABLE customers (
        id_customer int IDENTITY(1,1) NOT NULL PRIMARY KEY,
        customer_name varchar(150),
        customer_status int
         )
```

With the tables created, we can close the SQL Server manager.

Creating a PostgreSQL database

To create the database and its tables in PostgreSQL, I am using version 9.3, but you can work with that version or a higher one. We will connect to our server through **pgAdmin**:

With pgAdmin running, continue with the following steps:

1. Select and connect to the server listed in the **Object Browser**. If there isn't one, add one.
2. With a right-click on the **Database** list, select a **New Database...**:

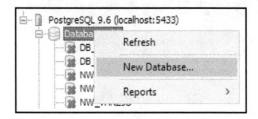

3. Set the DATABASE name to packt, the OWNER as postgres, and add a client_encoding variable to 'WIN1252' or 'latin1':

pgAdmin has a **Final** tab in the creation of a new database, which will display the SQL code used to create the new database. This should be according to the preceding screenshot.

Creating tables in PostgreSQL

Once you have the `packt` database created, you can create the `users`, `products`, and `customers` tables.

To do this, follow these steps:

1. Select the newly created database, `packt`, in the **Object Browser**, and click on the button to open a new query, as shown in the following screenshot:

2. Write the SQL code for the creation of the following tables:

   - The SQL code for the `users` table is as follows:

```
CREATE TABLE public.users
(
    id_user bigserial NOT NULL,
    login character varying(50),
    password character varying(50),
    CONSTRAINT pk_users PRIMARY KEY (id_user)
)
WITH (
  OIDS = FALSE
)
;
ALTER TABLE public.users
  OWNER TO postgres;
```

   - The SQL code for the `products` table is as follows:

```
CREATE TABLE public.products
(
    id_product bigserial NOT NULL ,
    code character varying(15),
    descr character varying(100),
    list_price float,
    tax float,
```

```
     quantity float,
     CONSTRAINT pk_products PRIMARY KEY (id_product)
)
WITH (
   OIDS=FALSE
);
ALTER TABLE public.products
   OWNER TO postgres;
```

- The SQL code for the `customers` table is as follows:

```
CREATE TABLE public.customers
(
   id_customer bigserial NOT NULL ,
   customer_name character varying(150),
   customer_status int,
   CONSTRAINT pk_customers PRIMARY KEY (id_customer)
)
WITH (
   OIDS=FALSE
);
ALTER TABLE public.customers
   OWNER TO postgres;
```

3. Run the queries to create the tables individually:

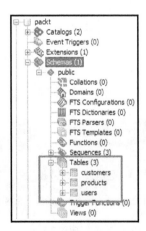

With the tables created, we can close the pgAdmin.

Models for a database – objects

To interact with a database (at least for what is being discussed in this chapter), we need a template, which will be the equivalent of the fields in the database tables.

The process is very simple. Let's create an object for each table in our database; regardless of whether it is SQL Server or PostgreSQL, we will only have one object per entity:

- users
- products
- customers

The users object

The idea to facilitate the maintenance and reading of the code is to separate a unit for each entity. In this case, we will need to create three new units for each table. To do so, follow these steps:

1. Open the Delphi IDE.
2. Create a new VCL project.
3. Create three new units (**File | New | Unit - Delphi**), and call them uUsers, uProducts, and uCustomers, respectively. Then, save them:

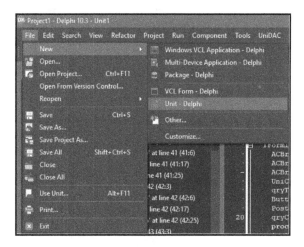

4. In Delphi, open `unit uUsers` and create an object based on the following code:

```
unit uUsers;

interface

Type
  TUser = class
    property id : integer;
    property login : string;
    property password : string;
  end;

implementation

end.
```

5. Use the combined *Ctrl* + *Shift* + *C* keys, and save.

Using the combined *Ctrl* + *Shift* + *C* keys will automatically create the getter and setter functions and procedures, as well as fill in the `private` objects, as they have been omitted in the declaration.

After using this key combination, your code will change; see the following example:

```
unit uUsers;

interface

Type
  TUser = class
    private
      FId: integer;
      FPassword: string;
      FLogin: string;
      procedure SetId(const Value: integer);
      procedure SetLogin(const Value: string);
      procedure SetPassword(const Value: string);
    published
      property Id : integer read FId write SetId;
      property Login : string read FLogin write SetLogin;
      property Password : string read FPassword write SetPassword;
    end;

implementation

{ TUser }

procedure TUser.SetId(const Value: integer);
begin
  FId := Value;
end;

procedure TUser.SetLogin(const Value: string);
begin
  FLogin := Value;
end;

procedure TUser.SetPassword(const Value: string);
begin
  FPassword := Value;
end;

end.
```

The `TUser` object, declared as `class`, has the `Id`, `Login`, and `Password` properties, and also the table structure.

The customers object

In the same way that we created the `TUser` object and `unit uUsers`, we will create `customers`:

1. With `unit uCustomers` open, create the object/class `TCustomer`:

```
unit uCustomers;

interface

Type
  TCustomer = class
    property id : integer;
    property name : string;
    property status : integer;
  end;

implementation

end.
```

2. Do the same with the key combination *Ctrl + Shift + C* to create the surplus of the class automatically and save the file.

The products object

In the same way that we created the `TUser` and `TCustomer` objects, and `unit uUsers`

and `unit uCustomers`, we will create `products`:

1. With the `unit uProducts` open, code the following:

```
unit uProducts;

interface

Type
  TProducts = class
    property id : integer;
    property code : string;
```

```
    property descr : string;
    property list_price : double;
    property tax : double;
    property quantity : double;
  end;

implementation

end.
```

2. Do the same with the key combination *Ctrl* + *Shift* + *C* to create the surplus of the class automatically and save the file.

In this way, we get an object-based mirror of the existing entities in our databases; whether they are SQL Server or PostgreSQL, the integer and `string` data types will be the same for both databases.

Our next steps will be to translate the newly created objects into objects linked to the database, either SQL Server or PostgreSQL, without having to create numerous configurations. For this, we will use interfaces.

Exploring Delphi interfaces

What do you imagine when we mention the word interface? Of course, there is a great possibility that you might think of a window/form for interacting with the users of your system. However, you can go deeper and also imagine the objects of our application interacting with each other. These, in turn, need to know each other, in order to know what messages they can exchange. This is where interfaces come in.

We can visualize the objects of our application as instances of a class in the memory and divide them into two parts—their external visualization and the implementation of their own methods.

Note that so far, we are only focusing our attention on this context. However, interfaces can be found in several other situations. In addition to the aforementioned user interactions and objects in between, entire programs can also communicate, and the hardware pieces need to fit perfectly. With this knowledge, it is easy to imagine several situations for the use of interfaces.

Let's conceptualize them as a contract between two parties. If an object declares that it implements an interface, it must follow it strictly, implementing everything stipulated by this agreement. In the same way, the other objects can be sure that the messages sent to it will be matched. And most importantly, they will know which operations can be requested.

Try to relate these objects with a program and its graphical interface. The intent of a form's drawing is to show what operations can be performed on that application, exposing them clearly to anyone using the system.

In Delphi, since we do not have multiple object inheritances, we also use the interfaces to ensure that certain objects implement features of other classes.

An interface only consists of method declarations. Its difference from a common class is that there will be no implementation in it.

Creating and using an interface

An interface, as we mentioned in the previous section, only consists of method declarations. To start our multi-database system, follow these steps:

1. Create a new unit and save it as `uiRepositories`.
2. In the new unit, below the line interface, enter the following line of code and hit *Enter*:

    ```
    Type
      IRepositories = interface
      end;
    ```

3. For now, save whatever is open, such as **Form1** and the project; give it whatever name you want.

    We will return the unit `uiRepositories` later; now, we need to create one more unit to work with the database tables.

4. Create a new unit and save it as `uiRepoSystem`.
5. In the new unit, below the line interface, enter the following:

    ```
    Type
      IRepoSystem = interface
      end;
    ```

6. In the `uses` of the unit, add the three units containing the table objects, according to the following code:

```
uses
    uUsers, uCustomers, uProducts;
```

7. Then, add three new methods inside the newly coded interface:

```
Type
    IRepoSystem = interface
        function ReturnUser ( id : integer ) : TUser;
        function ReturnCustomer( id : integer) : TCustomer;
        function ReturnProduct ( id : integer) : TProducts;
    end;
```

Note that the function call requests the handle parameter and returns the complete object. This is our object.

8. With the unit `uiRepositories` open, we can now include other information, and finally, we can reveal part of the secret. First, add the `uses` class:

```
uses
    uiRepoSystem;
```

9. Add the following method in the interface:

```
Type
    IRepositories = interface
        function Repository : IRepoSystem;
    end;
```

In our `uiRepositories` unit, follow these steps:

1. Before the declaration of the interface, we will create an enumerated `Type`, which will contain the types of supported database managers (in our case, SQL Server and PostgreSQL):

```
Type
    TpTypeRepo = ( trADOSQLServer, trUniPostgreSQL );

    IRepositories = interface
        function Repository : IRepoSystem;
    end;
```

2. After the interface declaration, create a signature function, as per the following code:

```
Type
  TpTypeRepo = ( trADOSQLServer, trUniPostgreSQL );

  IRepositories = interface
      function Repository : IRepoSystem;
  end;

function Repositories: IRepositories;
```

3. Continuing just after the implementation statement, create an interface variable:

```
implementation

var
  mRepositories : IRepositories = nil;
```

4. Finally, we will create the function, which is not linked to any class that will verify which database will be instantiated.

Before we proceed, it will be necessary to develop the two types of repositories for later configuration. We'll start with SQL Server.

Repositories

Repositories, by definition, are places to store data. However, in the pattern presented in this chapter, it has nothing to do with the GoF, nor does it resemble **Data Access Objects (DAO)**. In fact, we use this pattern as a separation layer where they will work with the database, regardless of the business rule, which will hold the managers or controllers in an MVC pattern.

Imagine the data module of Delphi, and imagine that Delphi, even being RAD, is fully object-oriented. Did you imagine the data module? Therefore, our default repository may even present itself with the data module, so we must separate the business layer, the view, and the management of the entire system from the database layer. This will become clearer in the coming sections.

SQL Server repository – part 1

Before we set up the repositories and work to their fullest extent, we need to create the objects to use the databases. Let's start with SQL Server.

In order to maintain the didactic rhythm, we will build the implementation queue for SQL Server in a data module. To perform connectivity, we will use FireDAC.

Here we go:

1. In Delphi, go to **File | New | Other | Database | Data Module**:

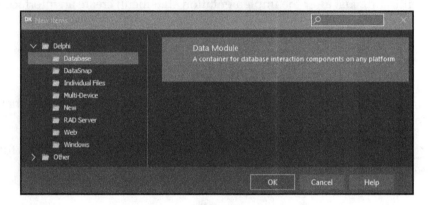

2. In the **Tool Palette**, look for the **FireDAC** connection component, **TFDConnection**. Add it to the data module:

3. Add the **FDPhysMSSQLDriverLink** component.
4. Now, you need to configure the database. Double-click on the **FDConnection** object that is added to your data module:

5. Put MSSQL in the **Driver ID** and fill in the fields for the server, user, password, and database. Use the parameters of your database manager, the same as you did for the tables at the beginning of this chapter.

6. In the **Object Inspector**, uncheck the **Login Prompt** option of the **FDConnection** component, so that you will not have to confirm the user and password every time that you connect.

7. Rename the **FDConnection1** object to `FDConnSQLServer`.

8. Name the `DataModule1` for `DM_RepositorySQLServer`.

9. Modify the unit name for `uDM_RepositorySQLServer`.

10. To code the least now, add the following units in the data module `uses`:

```
uses
    Forms, Dialogs, uiRepositories, uiRepoSystem, .....
```

 The ... (dots) after the comma mean that the rest of the units are the default ones, added by the other added components, such as FireDAC.

11. Now, it is necessary that when the application creates this data module, we program the connection with the proposed database. To do this, create a procedure that's unlinked from the main class (that is, a global procedure) in the context of the unit, after the end of the `Type` section:

```
procedure initialize; //declaration
```

12. With the statement made, let's implement it:

```
procedure initialize;
begin
   If Assigned( DM_RepositorySQLServer ) then
        exit;
   Application.CreateForm(TDM_RepositorySQLServer,
DM_RepositorySQLServer);
end;
```

13. Last, but not least, we need to encode the **OnCreate** event so that the `initialize` procedure makes sense:

```
procedure TDM_RepositorySQLServer.DataModuleCreate(Sender:
TObject);
begin
   Try
     FDConnSQLServer.Connected := False;
     FDConnSQLServer.Connected := True;
   Except
     On E : Exception do
       ShowMessage('Error Connect SQL Server : ' + E.Message)
```

```
    End;
end;
```

It's important to remember that in this step, we can set up the parameters of the database at runtime. In this example, we are only disconnecting and connecting to the current parameters, imputed in step 4 of this section.

In the `DataModule` class declaration, we will implement our repository interface. This will ensure that `DataModule` implements the interface methods shown in the next step.

14. Include the `iRepositories` interface in the `DataModule`:

```
type
    TDM_RepositorySQLServer = class(TDataModule, IRepositories)
```

15. In the `DataModule` `public` statement, try using the *Ctrl* + spacebar shortcut key. Delphi will display the functions and procedures of the interface so that you can implement them. However, if you need to inform on this manually, enter the following:

```
public
    function Repository: IRepoSystem;
```

16. Use the shortcut *Ctrl* + *Shift* + *C* to create the implementation of this function, and save the project.

SQL Server repository – part 2

We have come to a point in the project where it will be necessary to implement the methods of the `iRepoSystem` interface, in the same way that we did with `iRepositories`. The `iRepoSystem` interface contains the signatures of the methods that will, in principle, recover the user, product, and consumer. In our first implementation, we will do the same search of the database in SQL Server.

To continue with the development and for educational purposes, create a new data module, adding the instructions that will implement the methods of the iRepoSystem interface, by following these steps:

1. In Delphi, go to **File | New | Other | Delphi Files | Data Module**.
2. Name the new uRepositorySystemSQLServer data module unit.
3. Now, place the name of the data module, which is DataModule1, for DM_RepositorySystemSQLServer.
4. Add the uses, as follows:

```
uses
    Dialogs, uDM_RepositorySQLServer, uiRepoSystem, uCustomers,
uUsers, uProducts
```

5. Save this under the name uRepositorySystemSQLServer.pas.

In the DataModule class declaration, we will implement our repository interface. This will ensure that the DataModule implements the interface methods. Follow these steps:

1. Include the iRepoSystem interface in the DataModule:

```
type
    TDM_RepositorySystemSQLServer = class(TDataModule, IRepoSystem)
```

2. In the data module public section, try using the *Ctrl* + spacebar shortcut key. Delphi will display the functions and procedures of the interface so that you can implement them. However, if you need to inform on this manually, enter the following:

```
public
  { Public declarations }
  function ReturnCustomer(id: Integer): TCustomer;
  function ReturnProduct(id: Integer): TProducts;
  function ReturnUser(id: Integer): TUser;
```

3. Use the shortcut keys *Ctrl + Shift + C* to create the implementation of this function:

```
30  { TDM_RepositorySystemSQLServer }

   function TDM_RepositorySystemSQLServer.ReturnCustomer(id: Integer): TCustomer;
   begin
34
   end;

   function TDM_RepositorySystemSQLServer.ReturnProduct(id: Integer): TProducts;
   begin
40 end;

   function TDM_RepositorySystemSQLServer.ReturnUser(id: Integer): TUser;
   begin

   end;

   end.
```

4. Now that we have declared the main functions and that we are working on a data module, we need to add the query objects to interact with the database. Start by adding a **TFDQuery** component:

5. In your data module, select the newly added query and rename it to `QryCustomerSQLServer`.

6. Open the `uDM_RepositorySQLServer` unit.

7. With the component selected, modify the **Connection** property for **FDConnSQLServer**, which is in the other data module:

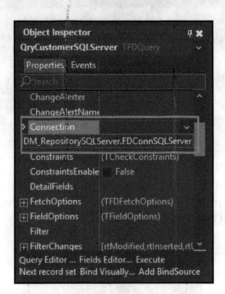

8. With the defined connection object, we can write our SQL code through the **SQL** property:

```
SELECT id_customer, customer_name, customer_status from customers
where id_customer =:id
```

If you double-click on the **Query** component, **FireDAC** will display a new window containing component information, including the SQL text to be entered and the parameter settings:

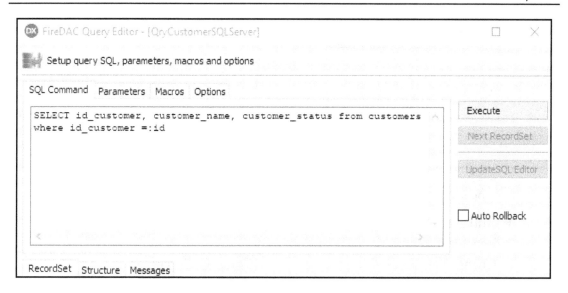

9. It is necessary to configure the parameter type (string, integer, and so on); otherwise, you will get an error message. To do this, go to the **Parameters** tab and modify the **Data type**:

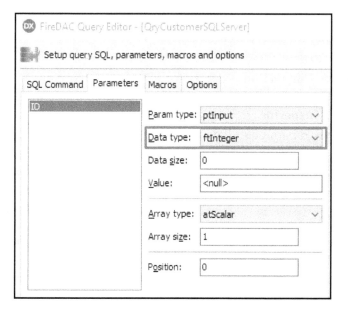

The following error message will occur when you run a query without the parameters being configured:

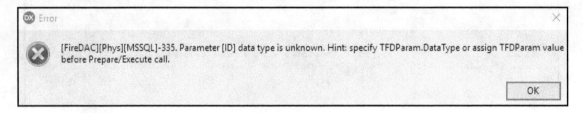

We will do the same for the other tables. Follow these instructions:

1. Add a new **FDQuery** component to the data module.
2. Rename it to `QryUserSQLServer`.
3. Change the **Connection** property for **FDConnSQLServer**.
4. Code the SQL sentence by using double-clicking, or by using the **SQL** property at the **Object Inspector**.
5. Modify the `id` parameter data type to the integer:

   ```
   select id_user, login, password from users
   where id_user = :id
   ```

6. Add another **FDQuery** component.
7. Rename it to `QryProductSQLServer`.
8. Change the **Connection** property for **FDConnSQLServer**.
9. Code the SQL sentence by using double-clicking, or by using the **SQL** property at the **Object Inspector**.
10. Modify the `id` parameter data type to the integer:

    ```
    select id_product, code, descr, list_price,
     tax, quantity from products
    where id_product = :id
    ```

The appearance of your data module should be as follows (more or less):

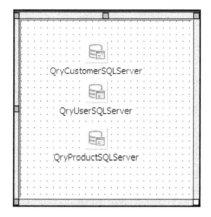

We now have the SQL codes prepared to search in our database for the customer, user, and product information, through an identification parameter: the ID. Therefore, when returning with the database information, we need to fill in the return objects and return this information to the system.

Let's go back to the code with *F12*, alternating between the code view and the form view. Let's encode the functions, as follows:

1. Code the `ReturnCustomer` function as follows:

```
function TDM_RepositorySystemSQLServer.ReturnCustomer(id: Integer):
TCustomer;
begin
  Try
    Result := nil;
    QryCustomerSQLServer.Close;
    QryCustomerSQLServer.ParamByName('id').Value := id;
    QryCustomerSQLServer.Open;

    if not QryCustomerSQLServer.IsEmpty then
      begin
        Result := TCustomer.Create;
        Result.id :=
QryCustomerSQLServer.FieldByName('id_customer').AsInteger;
        Result.name :=
QryCustomerSQLServer.FieldByName('customer_name').AsString;
        Result.status :=
QryCustomerSQLServer.FieldByName('customer_status').AsInteger;
      end;
    Except
```

```
    On E : Exception do
       ShowMessage(E.Message);
   End;
end;
```

2. Code the `ReturnUser` function as follows:

```
function TDM_RepositorySystemSQLServer.ReturnUser(id: Integer):
TUser;
begin
Try
    Result := nil;
    QryUserSQLServer.Close;
    QryUserSQLServer.ParamByName('id').Value := id;
    QryUserSQLServer.Open;

    if not QryUserSQLServer.IsEmpty then
      begin
        Result := TUser.Create;
        Result.id :=
QryUserSQLServer.FieldByName('id_user').AsInteger;
        Result.login :=
QryUserSQLServer.FieldByName('login').AsString;
        Result.password :=
QryUserSQLServer.FieldByName('password').AsString;
      end;
   Except
     On E : Exception do
        ShowMessage(E.Message);
   End;
end;
```

3. Code the `ReturnProduct` function as follows:

```
function TDM_RepositorySystemSQLServer.ReturnProduct(id: Integer):
TProducts;
begin
  Try
    Result := nil;
    QryProductSQLServer.Close;
    QryProductSQLServer.ParamByName('id').Value := id;
    QryProductSQLServer.Open;

    if not QryProductSQLServer.IsEmpty then
      begin
        Result := TProducts.Create;
        Result.id :=
QryProductSQLServer.FieldByName('id_product').AsInteger;
```

```
        Result.code :=
QryProductSQLServer.FieldByName('code').AsString;
        Result.descr :=
QryProductSQLServer.FieldByName('descr').AsString;
        Result.list_price :=
QryProductSQLServer.FieldByName('list_price').AsFloat;
        Result.tax :=
QryProductSQLServer.FieldByName('tax').AsFloat;
        Result.quantity :=
QryProductSQLServer.FieldByName('quantity').AsFloat;
      end;
  Except
    On E : Exception do
      ShowMessage(E.Message);
  End;
end;
```

4. Return to the `uDM_RepositorySQLServer` unit.

5. After the implementation line, add the `uses`:

```
uses
  uRepositorySystemSQLServer;
```

6. Create a new variable in the context of the implementation:

```
var
  mRepository : IRepoSystem;
```

7. In the function `Repository`, which was with its empty implementation, in *SQL Server repository – part 1* section, will now be encoded, to have the effect, add the following lines of code:

```
function TDM_RepositorySQLServer.Repository: IRepoSystem;
begin
  if not assigned(mRepository) then
    mRepository := TDM_RepositorySystemSQLServer.Create(Self);
  Result := mRepository;
end;
```

We will not mess with the SQL Server code again; its implementation is now complete.

PostgreSQL repository – part 1

The following content is very similar to what was passed to the SQL Server database. The components and the pattern will be the same; now, we will work with the PostgreSQL database.

Here we go:

1. In Delphi, go to **File | New | Other | Delphi Files | Data Module**:

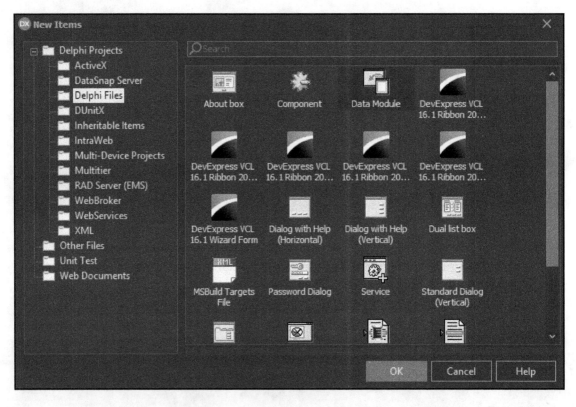

2. In the **Tool Palette**, look for the **FireDAC Connection** component, **FDConnection**. Add it to the data module.
3. Add the **FDPhysPgDriverLink** component.
4. Copy the `libpq.dll` driver to the application folder. See more details at `http://docwiki.embarcadero.com/RADStudio/Rio/en/Connect_to_PostgreSQL_(FireDAC)`.

5. Now, you need to configure the database. Double-click on the **FDConnection** object that is added to your data module:

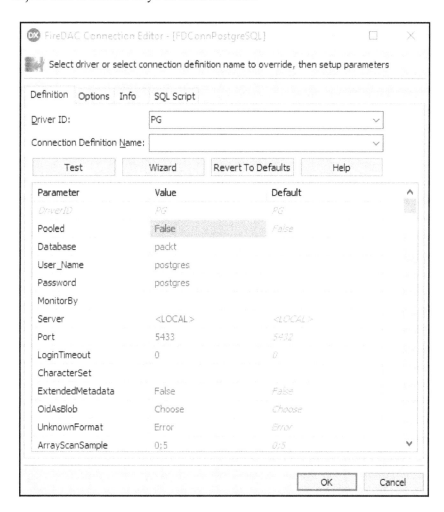

5. Put PG in the **Driver ID**, and fill in the fields for the server, user, password, port, and database. Use the parameters of your database manager, the same as you did for the tables at the beginning of this chapter.

6. In the **Object Inspector**, uncheck the **Login Prompt** option of the **FDConnection** component, so that you will not have to confirm the user and password every time you connect.

7. Rename the **FDConnection1** object to `FDConnPostgreSQL`.

8. Name the `DataModule1` for `DM_RepositoryPostgreSQL`.

9. Modify the unit name for `uDM_RepositoryPostgreSQL`.

10. To minimize the amount of encoding, add the following units in the data module `uses`:

```
uses
    Forms, Dialogs, uiRepositories, uiRepoSystem
```

11. Now, it is necessary that when the application creates this data module, we program the connection with the proposed database. To do this, create a procedure that's unlinked from the main class (that is, a global procedure) in the context of the unit:

```
procedure initialize; //declaration
```

12. With the statement made, let's implement it:

```
procedure initialize;
begin
   If Assigned( DM_RepositoryPostgreSQL ) then
        exit;
   Application.CreateForm(TDM_RepositoryPostgreSQL,
DM_RepositoryPostgreSQL);
end;
```

13. Last, but not least, we need to encode the **OnCreate** event so that the `initialize` procedure makes sense:

```
procedure TDM_RepositoryPostgreSQL.DataModuleCreate(Sender:
TObject);
begin
   Try
      FDConnPostgreSQL.Connected := False;
      FDConnPostgreSQL.Connected := True;
   Except
      On E : Exception do
         ShowMessage('Error Connect PostgreSQL : ' + E.Message)
   End;
end;
```

In the `DataModule` class declaration, we will implement our repository interface. This will ensure that `DataModule` implements the interface methods. Follow these steps.

14. Include the `iRepositories` interface in the `DataModule`:

```
type
    TDM_RepositoryPostgreSQL = class(TDataModule, IRepositories)
```

15. In the data module `public` statement, try using the *Ctrl* + spacebar shortcut key. Delphi will display the functions and procedures of the interface so that you can implement them. However, if you need to inform on this manually, enter the following:

```
public
    function Repository: IRepoSystem;
```

16. Use the shortcut keys *Ctrl* + *Shift* + *C* to create the implementation of this function, and save the project.

PostgreSQL repository – part 2

The development of the PostgreSQL repository, in this case, is very similar to what was previously codified for SQL Server; however, the great advantage is maintaining the characteristics of each type of database and the business rules, according to the user's needs.

To continue the development and for educational purposes, create a new data module, adding the instructions that will implement the methods of the `iRepoSystem` interface, by following these steps:

1. In Delphi, go to **File | New | Other | Delphi Files | Data Module**.
2. Name the new `uRepositorySystemPostgreSQL` data module unit.
3. Now, add the name of the data module, which is `DataModule1`, for `DM_RepositorySystemPostgreSQL`.
4. Add the `uses`:

```
uses
Dialogs, uDM_RepositoryPostgreSQL, uiRepoSystem, uCustomers,
uUsers, uProducts,
```

5. Save this as `uRepositorySystemPostgreSQL.pas`.

In the `DataModule` class declaration, we will implement our repository interface, like the SQL Server unit. Follow these steps:

1. Include the `iRepoSystem` interface in the DataModule:

```
type
    TDM_RepositorySystemPostreSQL = class(TDataModule, IRepoSystem)
```

2. In the data module `public` statement, try using the *Ctrl* + spacebar shortcut key, or code the following:

```
public
    { Public declarations }
    function ReturnCustomer(id: Integer): TCustomer;
    function ReturnProduct(id: Integer): TProducts;
    function ReturnUser(id: Integer): TUser;
```

5. Add three **FDQuery** components in the data module:

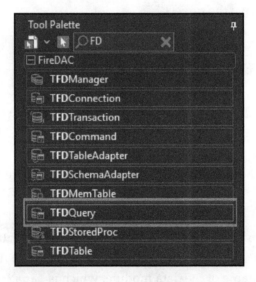

6. Select the three components on the screen by pressing the *Shift* key, keeping all the selected query objects.

7. Go to the **Object Inspector** and modify the **Connection** property for the connection to
   PostgreSQL, `<DM_RepositoryPostgreSQL.FDConnPostgreSQL>`:

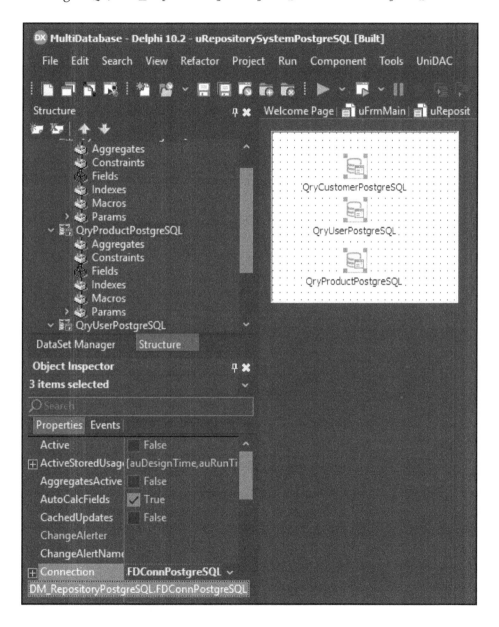

8. In our example, the ANSI SQL standard and the names of the tables and columns are the same, except that when you use a specific schema in PostgreSQL (`schema.table`), it is not recommended to copy SQL content. However, in this example, you can copy the content of queries without major problems. From the unit uRepositorySQLServer, copy the SQL content of each `FDQuery` component to PostgreSQL.

 Remember that when you are copying the SQL contents of the previous query, you will also need to configure the data type of the parameters of each query. In our example, the only existing parameter for each query is the `id`.

Let's go back to the code with *F12*, alternating between the code view and the form view. We'll do the same thing that we did for SQL Server, but for PostgreSQL. Let's encode the functions:

1. Code `ReturnCustomer` as follows:

```
function TDM_RepositorySystemPostgreSQL.ReturnCustomer(id:
Integer): TCustomer;
begin
  Try
    Result := nil;
    QryCustomerPostgreSQL.Close;
    QryCustomerPostgreSQL.ParamByName('id').Value := id;
    QryCustomerPostgreSQL.Open;

    if not QryCustomerPostgreSQL.IsEmpty then
      begin
        Result := TCustomer.Create;
        Result.id :=
QryCustomerPostgreSQL.FieldByName('id_customer').AsInteger;
        Result.name :=
QryCustomerPostgreSQL.FieldByName('customer_name').AsString;
        Result.status :=
QryCustomerPostgreSQL.FieldByName('customer_status').AsInteger;
      end;
  Except
    On E : Exception do
      ShowMessage(E.Message);
  End;
end;
```

2. Code `ReturnUser` as follows:

```
function TDM_RepositorySystemPostgreSQL.ReturnUser(id: Integer):
TUser;
begin
   Try
    Result := nil;
    QryUserPostgreSQL.Close;
    QryUserPostgreSQL.ParamByName('id').Value := id;
    QryUserPostgreSQL.Open;

    if not QryUserPostgreSQL.IsEmpty then
      begin
        Result := TUser.Create;
        Result.id :=
QryUserPostgreSQL.FieldByName('id_user').AsInteger;
        Result.login :=
QryUserPostgreSQL.FieldByName('login').AsString;
        Result.password :=
QryUserPostgreSQL.FieldByName('password').AsString;
      end;
   Except
     On E : Exception do
       ShowMessage(E.Message);
   End;
end;
```

3. Code `ReturnProduct` as follows:

```
function TDM_RepositorySystemPostgreSQL.ReturnProduct(id: Integer):
TProducts;
begin
  Try
    Result := nil;
    QryProductPostgreSQL.Close;
    QryProductPostgreSQL.ParamByName('id').Value := id;
    QryProductPostgreSQL.Open;

    if not QryProductPostgreSQL.IsEmpty then
      begin
        Result := TProducts.Create;
        Result.id :=
QryProductPostgreSQL.FieldByName('id_product').AsInteger;
        Result.code :=
QryProductPostgreSQL.FieldByName('code').AsString;
        Result.descr :=
QryProductPostgreSQL.FieldByName('descr').AsString;
        Result.list_price :=
```

```
QryProductPostgreSQL.FieldByName('list_price').AsFloat;
      Result.tax :=
QryProductPostgreSQL.FieldByName('tax').AsFloat;
      Result.quantity :=
QryProductPostgreSQL.FieldByName('quantity').AsFloat;
    end;
  Except
    On E : Exception do
      ShowMessage(E.Message);
  End;
end;
```

4. Return to the `uDM_RepositoryPostgreSQL` unit.

5. After the implementation line, add the `uses`:

   ```
   uses
     uRepositorySystemPostgreSQL;
   ```

6. Create a new variable in the context of the implementation:

   ```
   var
     mRepository : IRepoSystem;
   ```

7. In the function `Repository`, which was with its empty implementation, in *PostgreSQL repository – part 1* section, will now be encoded, to have the effect, add the following lines:

   ```
   function TDM_RepositoryPostgreSQL.Repository: IRepoSystem;
   begin
     if not assigned(mRepository) then
       mRepository := TDM_RepositorySystemPostgreSQL.Create(Self);
     Result := mRepository;
   end;
   ```

There is nothing left to program for the PostgreSQL repository at the moment. Now, we need to configure which database we will use. For this, we will have a configurator based on the singleton.

Singleton

A **singleton** ensures that a class will only have one instance and will provide a single global access point that's the same. It may be one of the simplest design patterns to implement.

The singleton will precisely ensure that you work with a single object globally throughout the project, using the same memory address.

We will be using a singleton, as this will be a great way to work in conjunction with the interfaces and ensure the smooth operation of our multiple databases without affecting memory management.

Nothing is better than learning in practice, so let's implement our singleton.

Follow these steps to create the configuration of our system:

1. In Delphi, go to **File** | **New** | **Unit**.
2. After the interface line, enter the following code:

```
interface

  Type
  IConfig = interface
    procedure setTypeDataBase(const Value : Integer);
    function getTypeDataBase : Integer;
    property TypeDataBase : Integer read getTypeDataBase write
setTypeDataBase;
  end;
```

3. Modify the unit name from **Unit1** to `uiConfig`.
4. Save the unit.

The first step in the configuration is the creation of our `iConfig` interface. This interface will allow you to have several other ways to get your configuration in the future, with respect to the visual layer, the call to the properties (or fields), and so on, without interfering in the specific implementation type. It doesn't matter if your configuration is received by reading a text/INI file, the windows registry, a database, REST API, or web service. The sky is the limit!

Now that we have the encoded interface, we will create a new implementation layer with only one property, which is the type of database being used. In this case, it will be reading an INI file.

Please follow these steps:

1. Create a new unit with the name `uConfiguration`.
2. In the `uses` clause of the interface, define the following:

```
uses
  uiConfig;
```

3. Create a new class called `TConfig`; this class will implement the methods of our `iConfig` interface. See the following statement:

```
Type
  TConfig = class(TInterfacedObject, IConfig)
  private
    fTypeDataBase : Integer;
  public
    function getTypeDataBase: Integer;
    procedure setTypeDataBase(const Value: Integer);
    Constructor Create;
  end;
```

TIP

What will characterize a class that implements an interface is the use of the reserved word `TInterfacedObject`, followed by a comma with the name of the interfaces (yes, you can use more than one interface for a single object). If you want to use an object of the persistent type, **TPersistent** (this allows for other features), use the word `TInterfacedPersistent`, and in the Uses class, define `Classes`.

4. Press *Ctrl + Shift + C* to create the declarations of the get and set implementations, automatically.

5. In the `uses` implementation clause, define the following units:

```
uses
  SysUtils, IniFiles;
```

6. Create the following variables in the scope of the implementation of the unit:

```
var
  mConfig : IConfig = Nil;
  Ini : TIniFile;
```

7. At the end of the declaration of our `Type TConfig` class, create a declaration of a function unbound to the object (a function of the unit), as follows:

```
Type
  TConfig = class(TInterfacedObject, IConfig)
  private
    fTypeDataBase : Integer;
  public
    function getTypeDataBase: Integer;
    procedure setTypeDataBase(const Value: Integer);
    Constructor Create;
  end;
```

```
function configuration : IConfig; //function declaration (our
Singleton)
```

```
implementation
```

 The most important part of the preceding code is the declaration of the `Configuration` function, which returns our `iConfig` interface. The declaration of the class object and the word **implementation** is merely illustrative, and is used as a basis for identification of the correct location of this coding function declaration.

8. The following code snippet shows the variable declaration and the implementation of our singleton function—the `configuration` function:

```
function configuration : IConfig;
begin
  if not Assigned( mConfig )
    then
      mConfig := TConfig.Create;
    Result := mConfig;
end;
```

This is the main (and crucial) point for understanding this part of the chapter. What we have here is a function that, when invoked by the programmer, will check for the existence of the object/interface created in the memory during the execution of the program, through the method `Assigned`. If this returns false, it will trigger the creation of the `TConfig` object, which is an interface object of our `iConfig` interface. Then, the result of the function is the newly created variable with the newly created object. The ace in the hole here is that the second time the function is invoked, the invoked object will no longer need to be created, and by simply declaring the unit in any form, you will have access to the same object, practically in the global scope, with no need to create it and or destroy it on each form.

9. Code the `Create` constructor event, as follows:

```
constructor TConfig.Create;
begin
  Ini := TIniFile.Create(ExtractFilePath(ParamStr(0)) +
'Packt.ini');
end;
```

10. Code the getter event, as follows:

```
function TConfig.getTypeDataBase: Integer;
begin
  Result := Ini.ReadInteger('PACKT','DATABASE',0);
end;
```

11. Code the event setter, as follows:

```
procedure TConfig.setTypeDataBase(const Value: Integer);
begin
  Ini.WriteInteger('PACKT','DATABASE',Value);
  fTypeDataBase := Value;
end;
```
Save this project. With this encoding, we allow the programmer to read and write to an INI file by simply calling the singleton Configuration.TypeDatabase.

Since we have everything that's necessary to implement the individual call of the repositories, we should return our unit uiRepositories to finalize the construction of our first singleton. Follow these steps:

1. Return to the unit uiRepositories.

2. In the uses section of the implementation, declare the following:

```
implementation

uses
  uConfiguration,
  uDM_RepositorySQLServer,
  uDM_RepositoryPostgreSQL;
```

3. From this, the function Repositories should look like this:

```
function Repositories : IRepositories;
begin
    If assigned(result) then
       exit;

    case TpTypeRepo( configuration.TypeDataBase ) of
      trADOSQLServer :
      begin
        if not Assigned(mRepositories) then
          begin
            uDM_RepositorySQLServer.initialize;
            mRepositories := DM_RepositorySQLServer;
          end;
        Result := mRepositories;
```

```
          end;

       trUniPostgreSQL:
         begin
           if not Assigned(mRepositories) then
             begin
               uDM_RepositoryPostgreSQL.initialize;
               mRepositories := DM_RepositoryPostgreSQL;
             end;
           Result := mRepositories;
         end;
   end;

  end;
```

At its initialization, the function is verified if the result is already known, that is, if the repository exists; if yes, it exits the function. Then, through the singleton function called `Configuration`, it is returned if the repository to be instantiated will be SQL Server or PostgreSQL. Since the parameter to be returned is an integer, it is possible to perform the typecast with the enumerated type `TpTypeRepo`, declared in the same unit.

We can work in two ways: with the initialize function for each type of database, or by creating the object for the variable `mRepositories`. In this case, we first use the dynamic creation with the initialize procedure, and once it's created, the return of the function will be the repository of the configured database.

Presentation and final testing

Our multi-database system is ready. We have the layers developed for SQL Server and PostgreSQL, and each database is activated according to an option in an INI-type configuration file.

Before we perform the implementation on the main form, we need to remove the **self-creation** mode data modules in the project settings, so that the application will control the form creation events. This is also important so that we do not have multiple unnecessary instances of our forms and/or data modules.

Data presentation

We need to ensure that all the work developed throughout this chapter can ultimately be consumed in the presentation layer of the system (form). The cherry on the cake is that you just declare some units in the form and reuse the code without interfering with the business rules (purely **object-oriented (OO)**).

To do this, follow these steps:

1. Go to **Project | Options | Forms**, and move the form from **Auto-create forms** to **Available forms**:

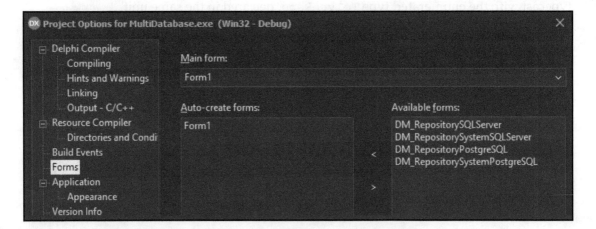

2. Confirm with **OK**. With the main form being **Form1**, the other forms/data modules are no longer in automatic creation.

3. Using the *Shift + F12* keys, select **Form1**:

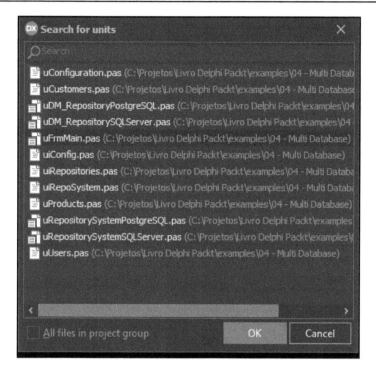

4. In the `implementation` section's `uses` clause, define the following units:

```
implementation

uses
    uiRepositories, uUsers, uProducts, uCustomers;
```

5. Add three **TButton** components to your form.
6. Modify the **Caption** property of the **Button1**, **Button2**, and **Button3** buttons to User, Customer, and Product, respectively.

7. Do the same with the **Name** property: `btnShowUser`, `btnShowCustomer`, and `btnShowProduct`:

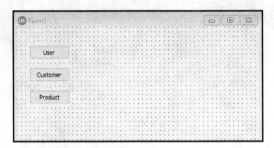

8. For each of the buttons, we will apply the code in your **OnClick** event, so that when they are pressed, a message with the complete object will be displayed.

9. The **OnClick** event of the `btnShowUser` button is as follows:

```
procedure TForm1.btnShowUserClick(Sender: TObject);
var
  pUser : TUser;
begin
  pUser := Repositories.Repository.ReturnUser(1);
  ShowMessage(pUser.login);
end;
```

10. The **OnClick** event of the `btnShowCustomer` button is as follows:

```
procedure TForm1.btnShowCustomerClick(Sender: TObject);
var
  pCustomer : TCustomer;
begin
  pCustomer := Repositories.Repository.ReturnCustomer(1);
  ShowMessage(pCustomer.name);
end;
```

11. The **OnClick** event of the `btnShowProduct` button is as follows:

```
procedure TForm1.btnShowProductClick(Sender: TObject);
var
  pProduct : TProducts;
begin
  pProduct := Repositories.Repository.ReturnProduct(1);
  ShowMessage(pProduct.descr);
end;
```

Note that for every test run of the display button, the **ID** parameter with the value **1** is sent in the fixed form. This is due to the fact that our example does not select a random register selected by the user, but rather a fixed record. For that, we have to feed our database at least one record for each table.

Remember that the INI file (`Packt.ini`) that we set for the database configuration will indicate whether the server that's used is an SQL Server or PostgreSQL, according to the enumeration (`0`: is SQL Server and `1`: is PostgreSQL).

> Use Management Studio on SQL Server or pgAdmin on PostgreSQL to enter dummy data into the `users`, `customers`, and `products` tables, to perform the tests.

In our example, the INI file is not created automatically; to create it, set a text file in the root folder of the main executable and modify the text according to the following screenshot:

Finally, you can compile and run your application and perform your tests.

Summary

Design patterns are a very widespread theme in technical literature, regardless of the programming language proposed. At the beginning of this chapter, a little bit of information about the concept, and various types of patterns (such as the creative, behavioral, and structural patterns and the GoF standard), were presented.

The theme of the chapter was then presented, and the challenge began—building a multi-database application with a little effort, using at least one design pattern and some interfaces in Delphi.

For the database, some servers were proposed: SQL Server Express and PostgreSQL. Database installation was not covered, but we demonstrated how to create new tables using SQL Server Management Studio and PostgreSQL pgAdmin with SQL scripts. A database named `packt`, with the tables `users`, `customers`, and `products`, was created; then, we need a class that represents the model. This is model is a representation of an object in Delphi for the corresponding tables in the database.

With the database and the basic model objects created, we arrived at the stage where we used the interfaces in Delphi to create other objects in order to define the repositories, and of course, the singleton design pattern was used.

The `iRepositories` interface was then defined, along with its `Repository` function, which would actually implement the selection of records in the databases.

Throughout the chapter, through the enumerated type `TpTypeRepo`, we could choose which database server we would use, depending on what was configured in the configuration INI file.

The singleton function `Repositories` was then displayed, and in this function, another singleton function, `Configuration`, was checked; it reads the enumerated type (`0` or `1`) from the INI file, defining which data is used.

For each database type, a separate data module was created by using the FireDAC connection components, and the data sealing of each previously defined table was made.

 Here's a valuable tip regarding the project options—remove from self-creation the units of forms or data modules that will be created dynamically by our application.

Lastly, this model is suitable for any type of database, independent of the database management system that's used.

In the next chapter, we will create a mobile application by using some material design rules and effects.

Further reading

For more information, you can check out the following links:

- Learn more about the project patterns in Delphi, including **object-relational mapping** (**ORM**), on the blog from Daniele Teti, also an author at Packt and MVP Embarcadero: `http://www.danieleteti.it/pages/dmvcframework.html#dmvcframework`

- Some example implementations of other project standards in Delphi are available on GitHub, from the developer Jaxx: `https://github.com/jaxx/delphi-design-patterns-examples`

5
Creating GUI Apps with FireMonkey

In 2014, Google developed a new version of its Android operating system and created a new design methodology, which was named Material Design. Nowadays, this is one of the biggest design trends. Designed to be fluid, natural, intuitive, and simple to understand, Material Design has several peculiarities and fundamentals.

Material Design aims to synthesize classic concepts of good design with innovation and possibilities brought with technology and science. It delivers a seamless experience across a number of different platforms, whether it be smartphones, computers, or smartwatches.

From enlightenment to how your animations will behave, everything is thought to resemble what would happen if it occurred outside the digital environment.

The Material Design guidelines are quite extensive. This is because its use is primarily geared toward application and site development, and so each interface element has its specific rule of color, movement, position, and so on. But even though it is so complete, all laws follow the same principles.

The material is simple, direct, concise, natural, intuitive, friendly, flashy, and kinetic. Each element of the interfaces goes and has to fit these characteristics.

The purpose of this chapter will be to develop a simple application with the concepts of Material Design using native Delphi components.

The knowledge that's needed to understand this chapter is intermediate—basic knowledge of functions, procedures, classes, and objects is required.

The following topics will be covered in this chapter:

- Creating Material Design layouts
- Working with animations
- Floating button

Technical requirements

To get started, you must have a version of Delphi installed on your computer. For the examples in this chapter, we'll use Delphi Rio, but you can use your version of Delphi as long as it's from Seattle 10 or later. You must have an Android or iOS phone to build the mobile application.

The code files for this chapter can be found in this book's GitHub repository: `https://github.com/PacktPublishing/Delphi-Programming-Projects/tree/master/Chapter05`.

Project overview

To build a rich interface, we will use the Google Material Design concepts and apply them using native IDE components.

The estimated build time is 10 minutes.

Getting started

Prepare your Delphi IDE and an image editor of your choice. We will be using Paint Brush to copy the color code in RGB format.

Creating Material Design layouts

Before we start building a layout, it is important to remember what was said at the beginning of the chapter—the concept of Material Design is not something plastered to a specific programming language. The concepts of Material Design are important and the theoretical part is essential so that you understand its entirety. The implementation of the concepts of Material Design in Delphi can be given through a menu, a button, a list, a form, and so on.

We will use the **Structure** panel a lot because it allows us to nest other components visually. In case you want to train on these concepts further, I suggest that you go back to `Chapter 1`, *Building an Instagram Clone*.

Material Design was idealized on the study of papers with ink, but is more technically advanced and open to creativity.

With this, the design becomes intuitive and easy to understand, since it is based on the reality that's lived outside the virtual environment and already familiar to users. At the same time, because it is more flexible than real materials, it creates new understandings that are not present in the physical world.

The objects that are present in Material Design have some immutable characteristics:

- They are solid
- They occupy unique spaces in the environment
- They are impenetrable
- Their shape is changeable (but can also be resized when at the same level as the Z axis)
- They are not foldable
- They can fuse to another object (at the same time, they can also break apart and mend)
- They can be created and destroyed
- They can move on any axis (X, Y, and Z)

Delphi has a wide range of visual components. With FireMonkey, you can build rich interfaces and further enhance the user experience.

With native components, it is possible to realize small wonders in visual terms. As our first task, we will create an application, and in this application, apply visuals and styles followed by Material Design.

First, let's put together a menu in a drawer style using the **TMultiView** component and then apply Material Design concepts.

To do this, follow these steps:

1. Open the Delphi IDE and start a new multi-device project by navigating to **File** | **New** | **Multi-Device Application**.
2. Select **Blank Application**:

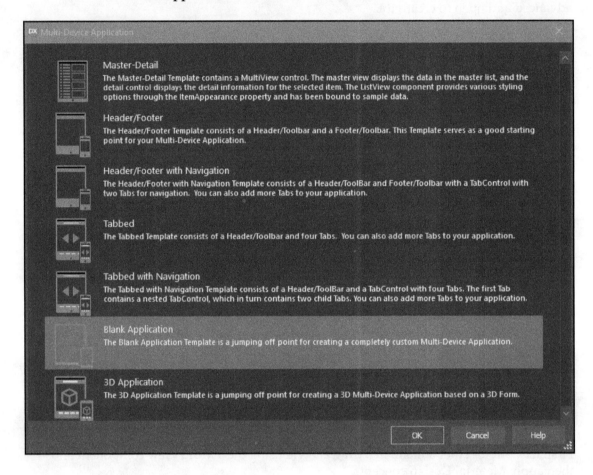

3. Add a component of type **TLayout** and align this to **Client**.

4. Add a **TRectangle** component and link it to the newly created layout. Do this using the **Structure** panel and align it to the top:

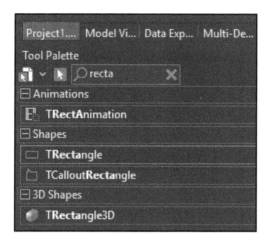

5. Add a component of the **TSpeedButton** type. This component must be nested to the first rectangle, aligned to the left.

6. Add the **TMultiView** component to the form. This time, the component must be bound to the form and not to the **TLayout**:

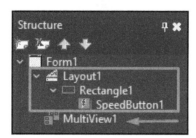

7. Modify the **Stroke.Kind** property to **None** in the **TRectangle** component.

8. Modify the **StyleLookup** property for **drawertoolbutton** in the **TSpeedButton** component:

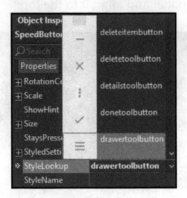

9. In the **TMultiView** component, modify the **MasterButton** property for the speed button that you added earlier.

10. Still in the **MultiView1** component, modify the **Mode** property for **Drawer**:

Now, let's save the project. In the next section, we'll build a menu in the best style of Material Design.

Using TMultiView

With the **MultiView1** component partially configured, we can enter the menu items. This is very simple—just double-click the component inside the **Structure** pane or right-click the **Show** option:

Let's build the menu items by following these steps:

1. Add a **TRectangle** component within **MultiView1**. Make sure that, through the **Structure** pane, the added rectangle is nested to the menu.
2. Modify the **Stroke.Kind** property to **None**.
3. Align the rectangle at the **Top**.
4. In the **Fill** property, click the arrow or the **...** button to open the image and color selection form, called **Brush Designer**:

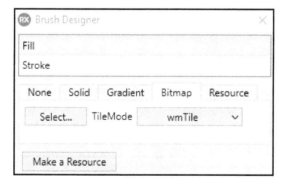

5. In the **Brush Designer**, go to the **Bitmap** tab and click on the **Select** button to select an image for our menu.

This step is very important, and the selected image should be the background of Material Design. There are several websites where you can download background Material Design files for free. For this chapter, the selected image is on GitHub and available in the examples folder of this chapter, or can be found through the following URL: `https://www.vactualpapers.com/wallpaper/material-design-hd-background-by-vactual-papers-wallpaper-49`.

6. In the **Bitmap Editor**, navigate to the image directory by clicking the **Load...** button:

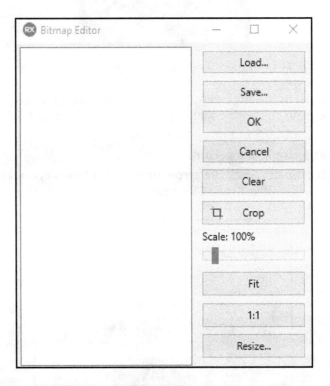

7. When loading the image, confirm the image that appears on the screen and, in the **Brush Designer** form, in the combobox named **TitleMode**, select the **wmTileStretch** option:

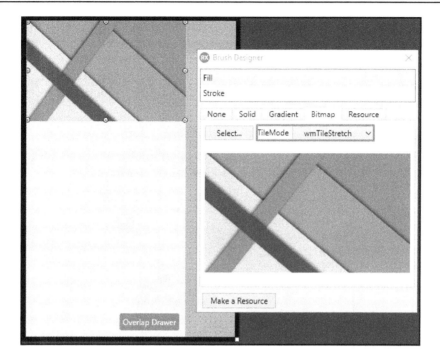

8. Modify the margins of this rectangle to −1 using the **Margins.Left** and **Margins.Right** properties.

9. Rename the rectangle to `rectMenuTop`.

10. Add a **TGridPanelLayout** component inside **rectMenuTop** and align to **Top.**

11. Using the **Structure** pane, remove one of the columns from the **TGridPanelLayout** by expanding the **ColumnCollection** tab and deleting one of the columns.

12. In the first row of the grid, add a **TCircle** component.

13. In the second row of the grid, add a **TLayout** component:

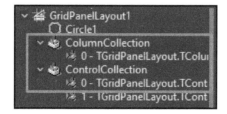

14. Align the **TCircle** component to the left, and in the margin properties, assign the values of 5 to the **Bottom**, **Left**, and **Top**.

> Through the **ColumnCollection** property, using the **Structure** pane, you can control which components are contained in which rows/columns.

15. In the **Fill** property, click the arrow and open the **Brush Designer** form. Assign a photo of yourself, as shown in the following screenshot:

16. Make sure that the option that's selected in the combo box is **wmTileStrech**.
17. Add to **TLayout**, which is in the second row of the grid panel, a label, aligned to the top.
18. Add another label to **TLayout** and align it to the top.
19. Modify the margin to 5 on the left, on the two labels.
20. In the first label, go to the **TextSettings.Font** property, modify the other properties, such as **Family**, **Size**, and **Font Color**, and assign the following values: **Roboto**, **15**, and **White**.
21. In the second label, use the same settings but set the size to **13**:

Your screen should look like the preceding screenshot, with the circle displaying the profile photo, followed by two text boxes: one to contain the user's name and the other to contain the user's email, or whatever they wish to enter.

Adding menu items

The menu in Material Design is almost ready. We can use an image to give the right proportion of geometric shapes in the background and insert a beautiful image inside the circle. It's time to include these options in the menu. Let's get started:

1. First, add a new rectangle and align it to the client.
2. Modify its **Fill.Color** property to **White.**
3. Modify **Stroke.Kind** to **None.**
4. Rename it `rectMainMenu`.
5. In order to keep the menu items in an infinity container, insert a new component inside the `rectMainMenu` called **TVertScrollBox**, and align it to the client.

 The **TVertScrollBox** component represents an invisible scroll box, and any component that is nested to it can scroll up or down, making it a sort of list. This is very useful for building menus in material format design, as well as forms with many fields to fill.

6. To create the first menu item, add a rectangle component by aligning it to the top.
7. Modify **Stroke.Kind** to **None.**
8. On the **Corners** property, deselect **Top Left** and **Bottom Left.**
9. On the **Fill.Color**, put **White**
10. Set the margins to 5 on the right and 3 on the top.
11. Modify the **XRadius** and **YRadius** properties to 15.
12. Add a component of the **TPathLabel** type to the rectangle by aligning it to the left.
13. Modify the margins to 1 at the top, 1 at the bottom, and 5 at the left.
14. Add a component of the **TLabel** type to the rectangle, aligning it to the left.
15. Modify the **Label** margins properties to 5 on the left.
16. In **TextSettings**, modify the font family and size so that they're **Roboto** and **13**, respectively.
17. In **Text**, put My Account.
18. Repeat *steps 6* through *16* three more times, thus creating three more items in the menu.
19. With four items in the menu, add a **TLine** component, leaving it between the last but one button, creating a divider, which modifies the **LineType** property to **Bottom** or **Top.**
20. Modify the **Text** property for the other labels inside the rectangles so that they show My Apps, My Camera, and My Books.

Now that all the menu items are present, we need to insert an icon that represents the functionality.

Using Material Design icons

As we saw in Chapter 1, *Building an Instagram Clone* the Instagram button was built using a SVG icon. We will use the same procedure to create the **TPathLabel** component.

For the first icon, implement the following steps:

1. Go to the following URL https://materialdesignicons.com/.
2. Select the desired icon of your choice.

3. Select the **View SVG** option:

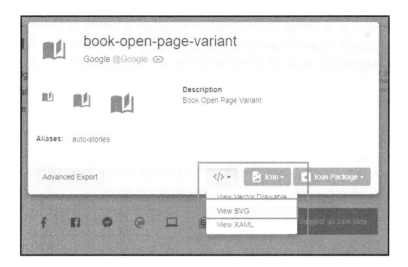

4. Copy the content that is in the d tag:

5. Paste this into the **Data** property of **TPathLabel**.
6. Modify the **WrapMode** property to **Fit**.
7. Modify the **Width** property to 2.
8. Repeat these steps for each required icon.

Your screen should look something like this:

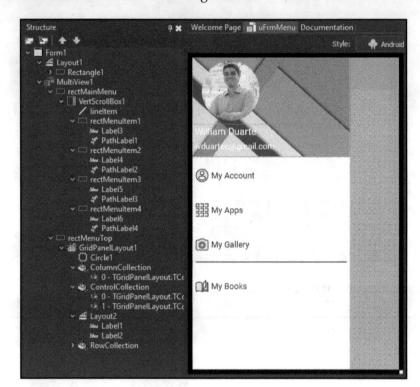

Use the preceding screenshot as a parameter for the construction of your form.

Colored effect

The menu is ready. Functionally speaking, if you want to compile your project and test it on the device, the menu will appear along with the items. However, we can improve it a little more by putting in some color. To do this, follow these steps:

1. Create an event associated with the main form, called `MouseMove`, with the following code:

```
type
  TForm1 = class(TForm)
    Layout1: TLayout;
    Rectangle1: TRectangle;
    MultiView1: TMultiView;
    .... more
```

```
    procedure MouseMove(Sender: TObject; Shift: TShiftState; X, Y:
Single);
```

2. Implement the code, like so:

```
procedure TForm1.MouseMove(Sender: TObject; Shift: TShiftState; X,
   Y: Single);
begin
   TRectangle(Sender).Fill.Color := $FFE0B4B4; //Color
end;
```

3. Create an event associated with the main form, called MouseLeave, with the following code:

```
    procedure MouseLeave(Sender: TObject);
```

4. Implement the code, like so:

```
procedure TForm1.MouseLeave(Sender: TObject);
begin
   TRectangle(Sender).Fill.Color := $FFFFFF;
end;
```

5. Link the MouseMove and MouseLeave events to the OnMouseMove and OnMouseLeave events of the rectangles that serve as the containers for the menu items:

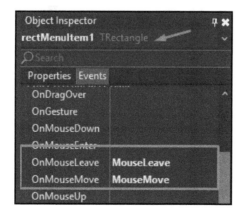

6. Save the project.

If you want to test the look of the application quickly and easily, you can generate it on a computer without any issues. Of course, the mobile experience will be much more enjoyable. This is what the form looks like:

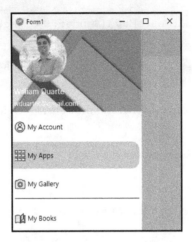

This is what it looks like on an Android device:

Working with animations

Animations on FireMonkey are awesome. Since they are easy to implement, they are perfectly adaptable to the movement style of Material Design.

The following table provides some examples of animations in FireMonkey:

Type of property	Animation Class
Any property that is an integer.	TIntAnimation
Any property that is a real number.	TFloatAnimation
Location of the component defined by a **TBounds** property.	TRectAnimation
Any string or integer property that contains a color.	TColorAnimation
A gradient (type **TGradient**).	TGradientAnimation
A bitmap picture.	TBitmapAnimation

An example of an animation of Material Design is the card. How about we include a card that expands and collapses when requested by the user? For this type of animation, we will work with layouts and rectangles, in addition to a very cool shadow effect.

Let's put the hand-in-mass, then:

1. Add a rectangle to the main form within **Layout1**.
2. Rename the rectangle `rectAnimate`.
3. Align this new rectangle as **alClient**.
4. Inside the new rectangle, insert a layout component, **TLayout**.
5. Now, align this layout as **alClient**.
6. Then, add a new rectangle, with the dimensions of 300px as the height and 260px as the width, to the new layout.
7. In this new rectangle, try positioning it at the center of your form.
8. In the **Fill.Color** property, change its color to **White**.
9. Add a shading effect by typing Shadow in the **Tool Palette** object search bar. This effect must be bound to the rectangle (use the Structure pane for this):

10. Within this new rectangle, create a **TLayout** component and align it to the bottom.

11. Inside this new aligned bottom layout, add a **Label** component.

12. Align the new label to the left and set a margin of 3px, also to the left.

13. Rename the new label lblCollapse.

14. Make sure that the **HitTest** property of lblCollapse is checked. Without this, you will not be able to activate the **OnClick** event.

15. Still inside the layout, add a **TLine** component, aligning it to the top.

16. Modify the **LineType** property from **TLine** to **Top**.

17. Resize the line so that it fits the label in the layout.

18. Finally, add a label, aligned to the top, outside the layout, bound to the rectangle rectAnimate.

This is what the layout will look like:

Use the preceding screenshots to guide you in building the layout. Notice that when you insert the **Shadow** component, shading becomes visible between the card and the desired effect:

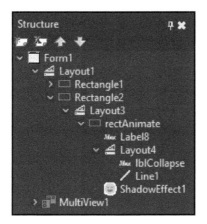

To finish and get the desired animation effect, we need to do a bit of coding:

1. Add the unit in the `uses` clause, `FMX.Ani`:

    ```
    uses
        FMX.Ani;
    ```

2. In the **OnClick** event of the `lblCollapse` label, use the following code:

    ```
    procedure TForm1.lblCollapseClick(Sender: TObject);
    begin
      if rectAnimate.Height = 300 then
      begin
        TAnimator.AnimateFloat(rectAnimate,'Height',100,0.7,
          TAnimationType.&In, TInterpolationType.Linear);
        lblCollapse.Text := 'EXPAND';
      end
      else
        begin
            TAnimator.AnimateFloat(rectAnimate,'Height',300,0.7,
          TAnimationType.&In, TInterpolationType.Linear);
        lblCollapse.Text := 'COLLAPSE';
        end;
    end;
    ```

The `TAnimator` static class is being used to call the `AnimateFloat` procedure, whose function is to animate a numeric property, which in our case is `'Height'`.

3. The required parameters are the components that you want the animation effect on, the property, the value you want to animate, and the animation speed. From here, you can define the type of animation and the type of interpolation. In mathematics, **interpolation** is a method that allows you to construct a new set of data from a discrete set of previously known data points:

```
TAnimationType = (&In, Out, InOut);
TInterpolationType = (Linear, Quadratic, Cubic, Quartic,
Quintic, Sinusoidal, Exponential, Circular, Elastic, Back,
Bounce);
```

Try other types of tweening in your code to see the different types of animation that are available.

You can use effects and animations for various types of objects, including images. How about going back to Chapter 1, *Building an Instagram Clone*, and incrementing your Instagram clone?

Floating button

A floating action button represents the main action of a form. This performs the main or most common action on a screen. It appears in front of the entire contents of the screen, usually as a circular shape with an icon in the center. They come in three types: regular, mini, and extended. Two floating buttons can be used if they perform different but equally important actions.

A floating button usually triggers an action on the current screen or performs an action that creates a new screen.

They promote important, constructive activities, such as the following:

- Create
- Favorite
- Share
- Start a process

Let's create a floating button on our system using native components:

1. Add a **TCircle** component (search `Circle`) to the form. This component must be linked to the form and not to any existing layout or rectangle.
2. Position your new **TCircle** to the right of the form.
3. In the **Anchors** property, only set **akRight** and **akBottom**.
4. Modify the **Stroke.Kind** property to **None**.
5. Set **Color** to **Fill.Color #FF127BAA.**
6. Add a new **TLabel** inside **TCircle** using the **Structure** pane and align it to the center:

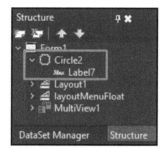

7. Enable the **HitTest** property of this new **Label**.
8. Put a + (plus) sign as the text of this label. Modify the **Text** property.
9. In the **TextSettings** property, modify the **Font** to **Roboto**, with a size of 40.
10. Finally, still in **TextSettings.FontColor**, apply a **White** color:

Action button

Note that because of the anchor properties, it doesn't matter if you resize your form. Your circle, or rather your floating button, will always follow the dimensions of the screen.

But there is still the main one: the action of the button. It will display another button of a different color, followed by an animation. Let's continue with the following steps:

1. Create a new layout using the **TLayout** component that's linked to the form.
2. Align this using the **alClient** option.
3. Create a circle component with the same measurements as the float button and bind it to the new **TLayout**.
4. Modify the layout name to `layoutMenuFloat`:

5. In the new circle, modify the **Fill.Color** property to **Red**.
6. Remove the border through the **Stroke** property by setting it to **None**:

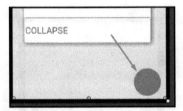

7. Set the **Visible Layout** property to **False**:

This is what the floating button should look like:

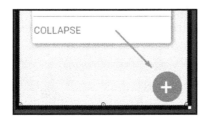

Note that by making the layout component invisible, the red button disappears.

Animate

We need to finalize the floating button implementation. The last step is to animate the click transition of the button, along with its onscreen placement.

It's as simple as what we've been doing already, so let's start coding.

In the label component linked to the float button, start an **OnClick** event:

```
procedure TForm1.lblFloatButtonClick(Sender: TObject);
begin
 if layoutMenuFloat.Visible = False then
  begin
    layoutMenuFloat.Visible := true;
    TAnimator.AnimateFloat(Circle3, 'Position.Y',
Circle2.Position.Y - 55, 0.4,
    TAnimationType.&In, TInterpolationType.Circular);
  end
  else
    begin
     TAnimator.AnimateFloat(Circle3, 'Position.Y',
Circle2.Position.Y, 0.4,
      TAnimationType.&In, TInterpolationType.Circular);
     layoutMenuFloat.Visible := False;
    end;
end;
```

First, the event checks whether the layout is visible or not. If it is not visible, the float button has not been activated. The static class `TAnimator` is then instantiated with the `AnimateFloat` function to modify a numerical property, which in this case is the Y position of the component on the screen, with a variation of 55 pixels above the normal button. With the circular effect and 0.4 seconds of circular transition, the button slides smoothly.

Summary

Graphical interfaces and user experience have been excellent topics to cover. The implementation of layouts using the concepts of Material Design is to provide the user with a rich, simple, and objective application.

At the beginning of this chapter, we presented basic concepts of Material Design and a little bit of information about how Material Design works. Then, we started by implementing a menu in the style of Gmail. The **TMultiView** component abstracts entire functions of style shadows and animation, which is fantastic.

In Delphi, we can basically build any layout using lines, rectangles, circles, and containers (layouts, grid layouts, and so on). By designing a card-style box that expands and collapses at the click of a button, we also implement a Material Design.

The transition is made smooth with `TAnimator` and effects, which serve filters like **Shadow** to make the application look even more interesting.

Finally, we ended with a simple floating button, which we made with two circles and a layout.

In the next chapter, we will learn how to create an app tethering application, open a remote application, and how to take a picture on a mobile and display it on the desktop.

Further reading

The best study guide for Google Material Design, undoubtedly, is the official website: https://material.io/.

6
Implementing Tethering to Create a Remote Control

App tethering is the name given to a Delphi feature that provides more direct interactivity between applications of the most varied types, developed under the context of the IDE.

App Tethering is one of the features that was introduced in RAD Studio XE6. App tethering allows you to connect applications in so-called serverless mode. That is, it gives your applications the ability to interact with others running on the same machine, or on a remote machine (such as a mobile phone), without using a server, as the applications communicate directly with each other.

A Delphi application developed with app tethering support is enabled to operate on three essential points:

- The first one is the location of other applications that also use app tethering, which are operating in the same execution context, the so-called **group**. Specifically, such a context refers to the device (or connected devices) wherein an application is running along with other applications.
- The second point is the execution of remote actions, instantly published by a particular application tethering and remotely invoked by others, which may or may not use triggers.
- The third point refers to the sharing of data and information between applications, in the form of resources (VCL or FMX). Here, support is currently provided for both traditional data types and streams.

In this chapter, we will introduce the concept and construction of app tethering applications, covering the following topics:

- Creating app tethering applications
- Sharing screens
- Opening applications remotely

Technical requirements

To get started, you must have a version of Delphi installed on your computer. For our examples, we'll use Delphi Rio, but you can use your version of Delphi, as long as it's from Seattle 10 or later. You must have an Android or iOS phone to build the mobile application.

The code files for this chapter are present on GitHub, at `https://github.com/PacktPublishing/Delphi-Programming-Projects/tree/master/Chapter06`.

Project overview

To build an efficient remote control, we will use an Android device to send and receive requests from a PC, both on the same Wi-Fi network.

The estimated build time is 15 minutes.

Getting started

Get your Android phone and a USB cable, activate your Wi-Fi network, and open the Delphi IDE.

Creating app tethering applications

In an increasingly competitive world, having a positive differential puts us ahead. Imagine being able to extend your desktop applications and control them remotely. It may be possible, for example, to develop an application that advances the slides of a PowerPoint presentation to you on your phone, without the need for any specific hardware.

If we think about it a little, extending an application leads us to building new solutions without the end customer wasting time (after all, time is money, oh yeah!).

Imagine a remote control; now, imagine your cell phone as a remote control for your notebook. We can think of some useful commands, as follows:

- Computer, open the browser on site *x*.
- Computer, turn off Windows sound.
- Computer, turn off the monitor.
- Computer, play a song.
- Computer, send me the sales report from my store.
- Computer, make a backup of the x folder.

Now that we know a few uses for the technology and we know a little about the app tethering technology itself, let's see some features, as follows:

- Full compatibility with VCL and FMX frameworks
- Availability for Windows (VCL and FMX), macOS, iOS, and Android (FMX)
- Native support for Bluetooth and a local area network (Wi-Fi)

 Bluetooth functionality is not available on iOS.

In this case, there is no client or server application; the devices communicate with each other, as previously reported. In terms of the client/server, there is no single role defined; all clients and servers communicate at the same time.

To develop a solution with support for app tethering, just use the following components and functionalities:

- **TTetheringManager**
- **TTetheringAppProfile**

Using app tethering components

Having introduced a little about the concepts and characteristics of app tethering, let's go to Delphi:

1. Create a new FMX project under **File | New | Multi-Device Application | Blank Application.**
2. Add **TTetheringManager** at the form.

3. Add **TTetheringAppProfile** at the form:

4. In the **TTetheringAppProfile**, modify the **Group** property to the value `Packt`. It is recommended that in projects in production, you use a group as the GUID (unique identifier).

5. In **TTetheringAppProfile**, link **TetheringManager1** in the component's **Manager** property.

6. In **TetheringManager1**, set a password by using the **Password** property in the **Manager** component. Here, I've set the password to `delphi`.

7. In the **AllowedAdapters** property, leave **Network** as an option, because we will connect the devices using the Wi-Fi network.

 As you add the components through the **Tool Palette**, Delphi automatically inserts the units into the form. However, if you need to create the components at runtime, the units are: `IPPeerClient`, `IPPeerServer`, `System.Tether.Manager`, and `System.Tether.AppProfile`.

8. In the `uses` clause, which is already in the implementation section, define the following new unit:

```
implementation

{$R *.fmx}

uses
  System.Tether.NetworkAdapter;
```

9. Go to the **Manager** component, and in the events, set the following code for the **OnRequestManagerPassword** event:

```
procedure TFrmCap6.TetheringManager1RequestManagerPassword(
  const Sender: TObject; const ARemoteIdentifier: string; var
Password: string);
begin
  Password := 'delphi';
end;
```

10. Insert a component, **TImage**, into the form, and align it to the **client:**

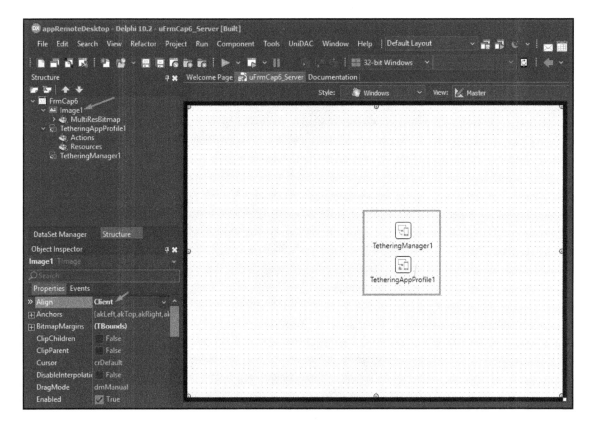

11. In the **Object Inspector**, in the **AppProfile** component, add a **Resource** by double-clicking on the **Resources** property.

12. With the added feature, set a name in the **Name** property; type Photo.

13. For the **Kind** option, modify it to **Mirror**, because in this case, we want the photo to be displayed here.

14. In the **ResType** property, set **Stream**:

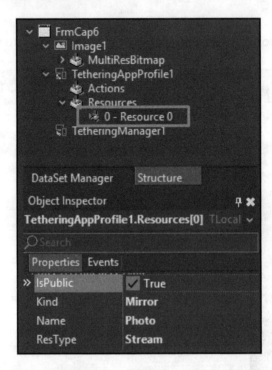

15. Finally, go to the **Events** of this particular resource:

16. Code an event, as follows:

```
procedure TFrmCap6.TetheringAppProfile1Resources0ResourceReceived(
  const Sender: TObject; const AResource: TRemoteResource);
begin
  TThread.Synchronize(nil, procedure
   begin
    Try
      AResource.Value.AsStream.Position := 0;
      Image1.Bitmap.LoadFromStream(AResource.Value.AsStream);
      image1.Repaint;
    Except

    End;
   end);
end;
```

16. Save your application.

For now, nothing else is needed here. Let's go to the mobile.

Sharing screens

Now that we have built part of the desktop application, we need to start developing the Android mobile application. In it, we will use the camera to send a newly taken photo, remotely and automatically, to the desktop.

Sending data from a mobile to a desktop

Start a new project in Delphi by following these steps:

1. Navigate to **File** | **New** | **Multi-Device Application - Delphi**.

2. Select **Blank Application**:

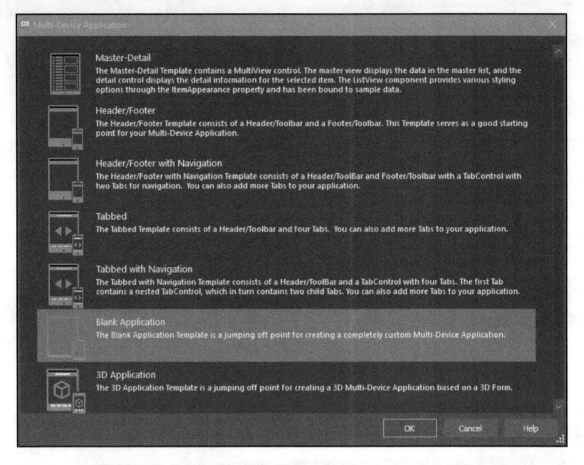

3. Add the **TTetheringManager** component.
4. Add the **TTetheringAppProfile** component.
5. In the **AppProfile**, go to the **Group** property; set the same value that you set for the desktop profile. In our case, we used the group Packt:

6. Set the **Manager** property for the **TetheringManager1** that was added to the form.

7. In **Manager**, set the password to the same value that you used on the server (in our case, `delphi`).

8. In **Profile**, add a resource in the same way that you added one in the desktop application, using the **Structure** panel.

9. This time, the feature set will be different; set **Kind** to the **Shared** property, rather than the **Mirror** that was made on the desktop:

10. Add a component of the type **ActionList** to the form.
11. Create a new default action; right-click on the **ActionList**, access the **Action List Editor**, and then define a new standard action:

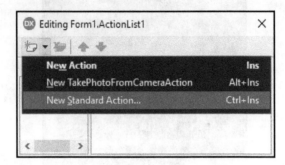

12. From the **Media Library** list, choose the **TTakePhotoFromCamera** action:

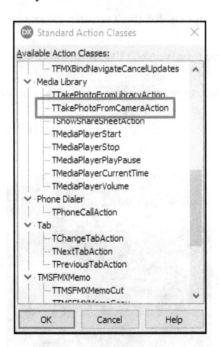

13. Create a new variable in the `private` scope of the form:

```
private
  { Private declarations }
  PhotoStream : TMemoryStream;
```

14. In the newly created action, go to the events and code the **onDidFinishTaking** event:

```
procedure TForm1.TakePhotoFromCameraAction1DidFinishTaking(Image:
TBitmap);
begin
  if PhotoStream = nil then
    PhotoStream := TMemoryStream.Create;

  Try
    PhotoStream.Position := 0;
    Image.SaveToStream(PhotoStream);
    PhotoStream.Position := 0;
    TetheringAppProfile1.Resources.Items[0].Value := PhotoStream;
  Except
    On E : Exception do
    ShowMessage(E.Message);
  End;
end;
```

15. Add two new buttons to the form: one to connect, and another to perform the action that will call the camera.

16. On the first button, set the text as `Connect`.

17. Below the first button, set the name of the second button as `Take Photo`.

18. Next to the `Connect` button, add a label so that we know whether it is connected:

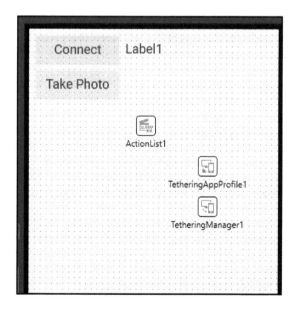

19. Now, let's program a little. Start by creating a `private` scope procedure called `Check`, as follows:

```
private
  { Public declarations }
  procedure Check;

procedure TForm1.Check;
begin
 if TetheringManager1.RemoteProfiles.Count > 0 then
   Label1.Text := TetheringManager1.RemoteProfiles[0].ProfileGroup;
end;
```

20. In **Manager**, code the **OnEndAutoConnect** event, as follows:

```
procedure TForm1.TetheringManager1EndAutoConnect(Sender: TObject);
begin
  Check;
end;
```

21. Also in **Manager**, code the **onRequestManagerPassword** event, as follows:

```
procedure TForm1.TetheringManager1RequestManagerPassword(const
Sender: TObject;
   const ARemoteIdentifier: string; var Password: string);
begin
  Password := 'delphi';
end;
```

22. Don't forget to code the **Connect** button with the procedure of auto-connection:

```
procedure TForm1.btnConectarClick(Sender: TObject);
begin
  TetheringManager1.AutoConnect();
end;
```

23. As the last call, code the **onClick** event from the `Take Photo` button:

```
procedure TForm1.btnPhotoClick(Sender: TObject);
begin
  TakePhotoFromCameraAction1.Execute; //piece of cake ;)
end;
```

24. To finalize, define the following unit in the `uses` of the implementation:

```
uses
  System.Tether.TCPProtocol;
```

25. Save and compile this.

26. Make sure that your app is allowed to use the camera on the device. To do this, go to **Project | Options | Uses Permissions** and check the **Camera** option. Use the platform selector to select the device (Android or iOS) that you want, as well as the build form (**Debug** or **Release**):

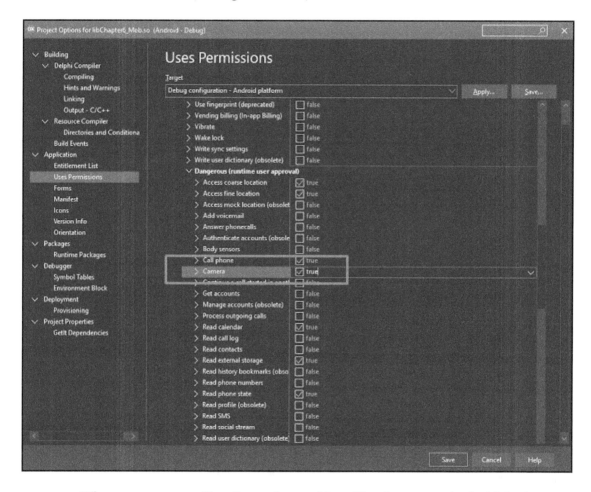

When you are compiling the project and installing it on your Android device, make sure that your mobile device is on the same network as your desktop computer. The adapter in **Manager** must also be network-enabled. Be sure to enable the permissions in the Windows Firewall, when prompted.

If you receive an error (**EIdCouldNotBindSocket**) with the message **Could not bind socket. Address and port are already in use**, don't panic; just click on **Continue**.

Run the app and take a picture; this is shown on the desktop application as follows:

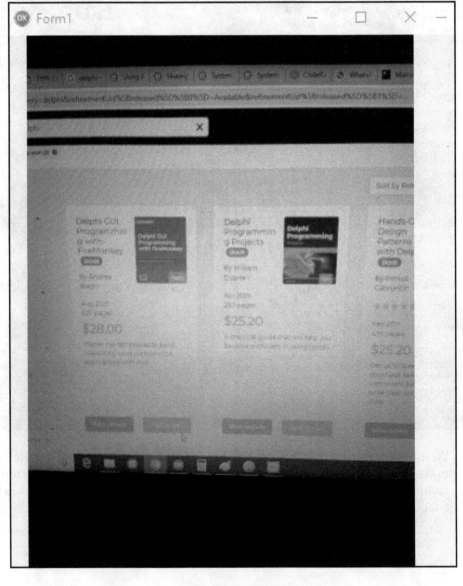

The following screenshot depicts the picture on the mobile application:

Taking advantage and giving thumbs up for you and also a small advertisement for the book already present in the desktop application.

Opening an application remotely

We have come to the point where we will evolve our application to perform an action remotely. Here, we'll add a new button to the mobile application, and a remote action will be triggered to open the Windows calculator.

Creating the desktop application

To proceed, open the desktop application project and follow these steps:

1. Add the following units:

```
uses
    Winapi.ShellAPI, Winapi.Windows;
```

2. Add an **ActionList** component.
3. Create a new action:

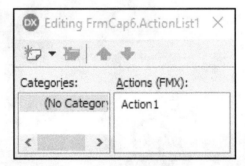

4. Select **Action1**, go to the **Events** tab, and code the **OnExecute** event:

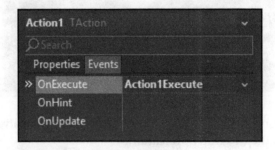

5. The code for the **OnExecute** event is as follows:

```
procedure TFrmCap6.Action1Execute(Sender: TObject);
begin
  ShellExecute(0,'open', PChar('C:\Windows\System32\calc.exe'), '',
    nil, SW_ShowNormal)
end;
```

In the same way that we added a feature (for the photo) in a tethering application, we can perform remote actions through an **ActionList**.

Let's finalize the construction of the desktop server application; follow the next steps.

6. In the **AppProfile** component, check the **Actions** tab in the **Structure** pane. Add a new item in the **Actions** menu:

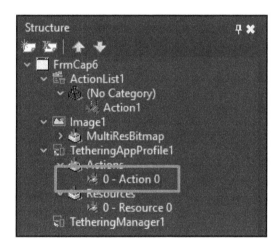

7. Select this new action linked to **AppProfile**, and set the name to `Calc`.
8. Select the action **Action1**, which we created earlier, in the **Action** property.

9. Keep the **Kind** set to **Shared**. This is very important:

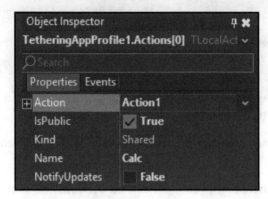

Now, the desktop application is ready.

Creating the mobile application

Once the action has been programmed, we will know that the **Action1** action control is already set to open the calculator, but it must be executed remotely. First, open the mobile application project and follow these instructions:

1. Use the existing **ActionList** in the main form and create a new action; this time, do not put anything in the code and just create the new action:

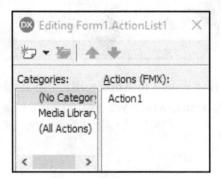

2. Now that the **ActionList** action is created, you need to create an action that is contained in the properties of the **AppProfile** itself. Add a new action by using the **Structure** pane:

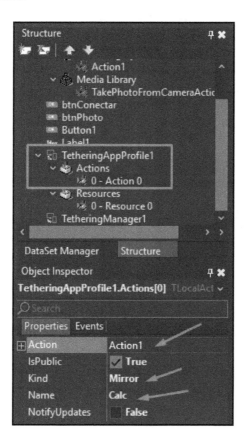

3. With the action created, link the **Action** property to its ghost action that was created as empty.
4. Unlike with the desktop application, leave the **Kind** property as **Mirror**.
5. Finally, use the same name that was also configured in the desktop application (`Calc`).

6. The cherry on the cake is to add a new button; enter your property name as `Open Calc`:

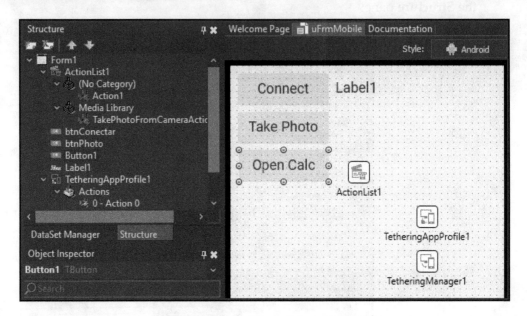

7. In the **Action** property of this new button, set the variable to **Action1**, so that upon clicking on the button, the remote action is triggered.
8. Save and run the server and client applications.
9. Click on **Connect** and wait for **Label1** to turn to **Packt**.
10. Click on `Take Photo` or `Open Calc`, and have fun:

Try some other actions; finding out whether your computer is connected to the internet (other than the network) is a good example. Another example would be controlling your PowerPoint by using your mobile phone.

Now, let's move on to the next chapter.

Summary

At the beginning of this chapter, you learned the basic concept of tethering technology and how easy it is to implement in Delphi.

This chapter was done in stages; we first created the desktop application, which we called the server, although it is important to remember that in app tethering, there is no concept of a client and server, since all of the objects can be clients and servers at the same time.

We were able to connect Windows and Android clients automatically, thanks to the **TTetheringManager** group property. Using the same group and the same passwords, the `AutoConnect()` procedure could then be used without problems.

Note that there is a difference between creating a resources in **TTetheringAppProfile** of the type **Shared** and the type **Mirror**, with **Shared** always being the origin of the information, and **Mirror** being where we want the effect.

It is necessary for the stream of this image to be loaded using an anonymous thread, because the bytes are retrieved in packets, causing the thread to solve the issue of drawing and capturing data upon receiving the new resource.

Finally, by definition, remote controlling consists of sending actions to be performed remotely, that is, without having to manually execute them on the main device. In Windows, we defined that the remote action would open the calculator, and that the mobile would be responsible for triggering this action. In order for this to work, first, the applications need to be connected; then, we use the **TTetheringAppProfile** action concept. Just like with resources, we can have **Shared** actions and **Mirror** actions.

By creating an action in Windows and assigning **OnExecute** with the trigger of the calculator, we defined that when the action is executed, the calculator will open. The interesting thing is that on the mobile, there is no coded action, just a link of a dummy action with the **Mirror** action of the **AppProfile**.

Therefore, every action generates a reaction. Once the empty action is linked to the mirrored action on the mobile, upon receiving the request, the button click will trigger the action event remotely to Windows, opening the calculator. Now, imagine the possibilities for remote access, even to back up your phone or by creating your own sharing screens.

In the next chapter, you will learn how to build microservices using the **RAD Server** (**EMS**), testing and securing the application, and eventually deploying and monitoring it.

Let's go to the next (and last) chapter, to learn about the RAD Server!

Further reading

For more information, you can check out the following references:

- **App tethering**: http://docwiki.embarcadero.com/CodeExamples/Tokyo/en/ RTL.BDShoppingList_Sample
- **PowerPoint with Delphi and app tethering**: https://www.youtube.com/watch? v=qiCljTF_z2o

7
Building Microservices Using the RAD Server

Microservices, or microservice architecture, is a systems architecture style that structures a solution as a collection of superficially coupled services that implement business features and facilities.

In a nutshell, microservices are a way to develop a solitary application as varied services. Each service runs in its own process and delivers the information through fluid mechanisms, frequently through an HTTP API.

Thinking about services the **service-oriented architecture (SOA)** and **Software as a Service (SaaS)**, we will use RAD Server as an application server for our microservice architecture and build a solution as a set of independent services.

In this last and final chapter, you will see the following topics:

- What is a microservice architecture?
- Introducing RAD Server
- Consuming services on RAD Server
- Securing
- Deploying

Technical requirements

You will need to have the Enterprise or Architect version of Delphi Tokyo or Rio installed on your computer. To distribute your application, a RAD Server license is required and **Internet Information Services (IIS)** should be installed.

The code files for this chapter are present on GitHub: `https://github.com/PacktPublishing/Delphi-Programming-Projects/tree/master/Chapter07`.

Project overview

To build our application-oriented microservice architecture, we will use RAD Server.

The estimated build time is 20 minutes.

Getting started

You must have an Enterprise or Architect version of Delphi and InterBase installed. To deploy, we use IIS.

What is a microservice architecture?

We will explain what the microservice pattern is by explaining the monolithic pattern initially—a monolithic application is made as a single part. Business applications are usually built in three main parts—a client interface (visual layer), a database (usually, a relational database system), and a server application. The server application takes care of requests, performs all processing, performs queries and updates to the database, and ultimately it sends data to the client's visual layer. This server application is monolithic—a single, logical, executable drive. Any change to the system is to publish a fresh version of the server application.

Why use a microservice?

In short, a microservice is a small, discrete program that provides business capabilities. It is independently deployable and almost always responds to an HTTP request with JSON.

By building a solution as a set of independently implemented services, we can present characteristics common to an architecture oriented to microservices as follows:

- Componentization
- Organized around business capabilities
- Products, not projects
- Smart endpoints and proxies

- Decentralized governance
- Decentralized data management
- Automation of infrastructure
- Plan to fail
- Evolutionary design

Monolithic application

Monolithic architecture is the most common and oldest operating system architecture, in which each system of the component is contained in the core of the system. It is an application made up of several modules that are compiled separately and then linked, thus forming a large system where modules can interact. The following diagram shows how **Monolithic** is different than **MicroService**:

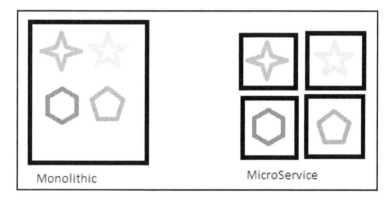

In the preceding diagram, each geometric shape represents a feature of the system. In a monolithic architecture, all functionalities perform within the same and unique processing. Besides observing the architecture of microservices, each functionality can be executed by a different process; each element is in a different service.

The original use of the monolithic term describes huge applications in the mainframe without usable modularity, thus resulting in unsustainable and crisis-susceptible systems in the software. Such monolithic applications are also commonly referred to as *spaghetti code*.

JSON or XML?

The microservices usually work with JSON to transfer requests and responses. It is obvious that it is possible to work with XML, but in REST architectures, it is required to use JSON. There are a few reasons at least for you to use REST/JSON in your microservice architecture:

- JSON is straightforward.
- JSON avoids tags.
- JSON means that data transfers are standardized.

By using **Simple Object Access Protocol** (**SOAP**) services, you must work with XML for data traffic. In addition, the code should be more detailed and XML data should be analyzed and validated. REST/JSON has come, in addition to simplifying and improving.

For a better understanding of REST architectures and JSON types, I recommend that you study Chapter 2, *Building a Facebook REST API* in this book, where we constructed the Facebook API service.

Introducing RAD Server

RAD Server is a set of solutions to create and deploy service-based applications (SOA, microservices, and so on) enabling developers to create new backends or migrate existing business logic to a modern, open, stateless, secure, and scalable service-based architecture. It can be distributed on a private Windows or Linux server, or in the cloud on Amazon, Rackspace, and Azure.

With RAD Server, there is no more need for you to build your own services and backend servers, you just load your Delphi methods into RAD Server and publish your backend code to any client, through REST/JSON endpoints. Embedded services and integrations provide the most common functionalities and access to the major external systems.

Before the RAD Server, developers had to create their own backends for Delphi applications, using tools such as DataSnap, which provide the basic building blocks for building multi-tier solutions, while leaving much of the work to the developer. With RAD Server, developers can simply load their methods with business rules, written in Delphi, add some users, and distribute. Endpoints are created and managed automatically. Access control is ready. Data storage is part of the infrastructure, or you can easily connect to any market database or even a cloud service. Track and respond to the user's location. Send push notifications to users. Integrate intelligent **Internet of Things** (**IoT**) devices into your solution and distribute in your infrastructure or in the clouds.

Starting with Delphi Enterprise, the installation already comes with a license for RAD Server development by default. This development license supports up to five users. To publish in production, it is necessary to acquire a license with Embarcadero. Delphi Tokyo 10.2.2 onward includes a single site license, obviously also from the Enterprise and Architect versions.

Where is RAD Server?

Some very common questions are, "Where is RAD Server? Is it installed? Is it part of the Delphi installation? Is it a plugin?" The answer is simple—the RAD Server is already installed in Delphi. To access your content, simply go to the installation directory of your Delphi, for example: `C:\Program Files (x86)\Embarcadero\Studio\20.0\bin`.

The main executables are as follows:

- `EMSDevServer.exe`: The development server.
- `EMSDevConsole.exe`: This is where RAD Server will show the analysis—what is being consumed, users connected, and so on.

The following screenshot shows the main executables:

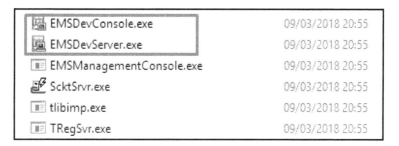

RAD Server stores the licensing information, connections, users, and so on in an InterBase database. Before proceeding, it is important that you, if you have not installed InterBase on your computer or Firebird, start the InterBase that comes with your Delphi installation.

To do this, follow these steps:

1. Navigate to the `C:\Program Files(x86)\Embarcadero\Studio\20.0\InterBase2017\bin` directory.
2. Open the `IBMgr.exe` program.

3. Start the service; it can be manual. If Windows Firewall appears, confirm the exceptions to running the program:

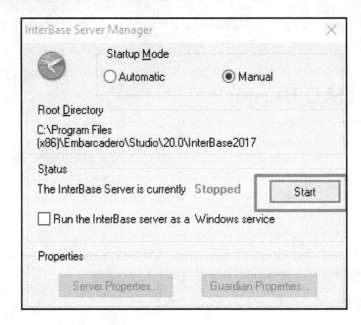

4. Check in the system tray to see whether **InterBase Guardian** is running:

 The InterBase path in the Embarcadero /20.0/ directory refers to the Rio version. For earlier versions, such as Tokyo, for example, the folder number will change to 19.0.

All set? You're fit to proceed.

Configuring the first project

To create a new RAD Server package, follow these steps:

1. Open your Delphi IDE.
2. Go to **Project** | **New** | **Other** | **RAD Server** | **RAD Server Package**:

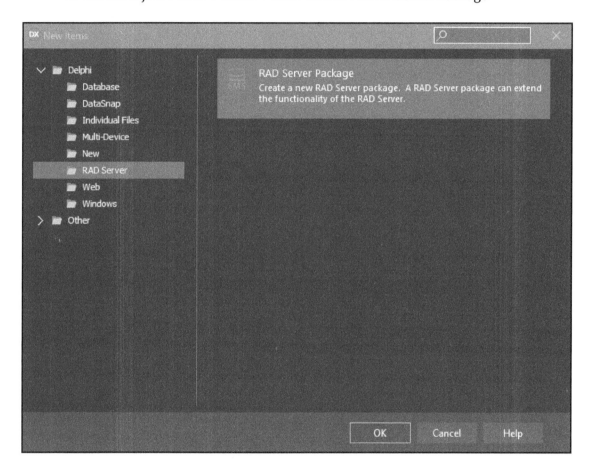

3. Select the, **Create package with resource** option:

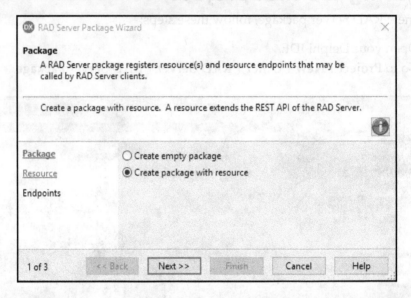

4. Fill in the name of the resource as `PacktExample` and check that the file type is a **Data Module**:

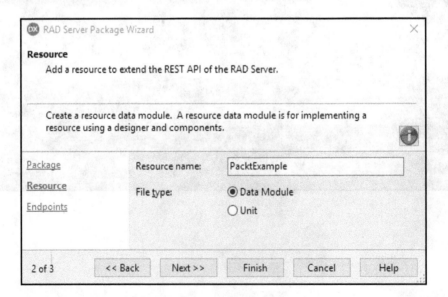

5. Click **Finish** to end the wizard.

Notice that, at this point, a sample application is created. Note that there is a `Get` method and that this method will return the string `PacktExample`:

```pascal
unit Unit1;

// EMS Resource Module

interface

uses
  System.SysUtils, System.Classes, System.JSON,
  EMS.Services, EMS.ResourceAPI, EMS.ResourceTypes;

type
  [ResourceName('PacktExample')]
  TPacktExampleResource1 = class(TDataModule)
  published
    procedure Get(const AContext: TEndpointContext; const ARequest: TEndpoint
    [ResourceSuffix('{item}')]
    procedure GetItem(const AContext: TEndpointContext; const ARequest: TEnd
  end;

implementation

{%CLASSGROUP 'System.Classes.TPersistent'}

{$R *.dfm}

procedure TPacktExampleResource1.Get(const AContext: TEndpointContext; const
begin
  // Sample code
  AResponse.Body.SetValue(TJSONString.Create('PacktExample'), True)
end;

procedure TPacktExampleResource1.GetItem(const AContext: TEndpointContext; co
var
  LItem: string;
begin
  LItem := ARequest.Params.Values['item'];
  // Sample code
  AResponse.Body.SetValue(TJSONString.Create('PacktExample' + LItem), True)
end;

procedure Register;
begin
  RegisterResource(TypeInfo(TPacktExampleResource1));
end;

initialization
  Register;
end.
```

The Delphi Wizard has added, in addition to the sample methods, everything necessary for RAD Server to work, including the units in the `uses` clause, which are as follows:

```
System.JSON, EMS.Services, EMS.ResourceAPI, EMS.ResourceTypes
```

By definition, a service on RAD Server is a **Borland Package Libraries** (**BPL**) library; you can check it through the **Projects** tools:

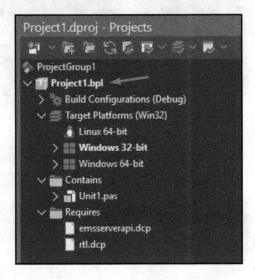

Leave everything as it is and try starting this project by using the **Play** button or the shortcut key: F9:

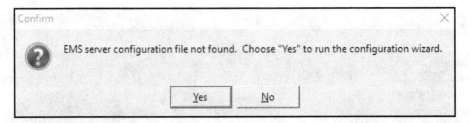

If this is your first time running a project on RAD Server, you will receive the message **EMS server configuration file not found. Choose "Yes" to run the configuration wizard.**

For a better understanding, follow these steps:

1. Don't fill in the **Server Instance** information; leave it blank. Fill this if your RAD Server is installed on another machine:

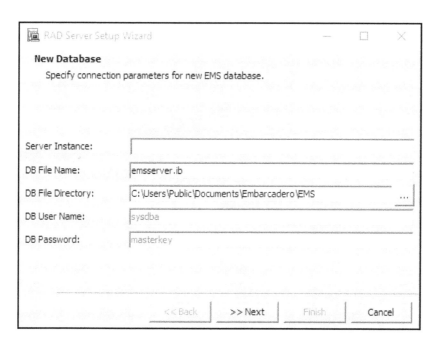

2. Leave the **Sample users** and **Sample user groups** options checked if you want to insert sample data into the database for users:

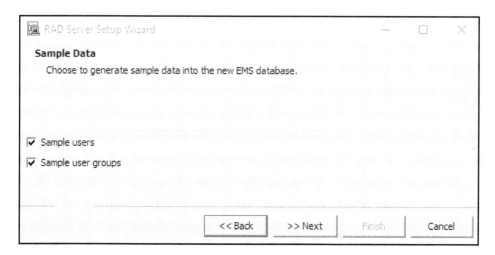

3. Enter a username and password for your server:

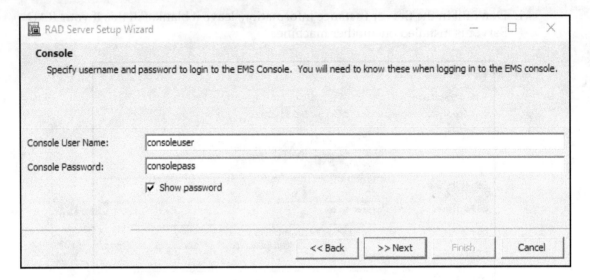

4. Choose **Finish**:

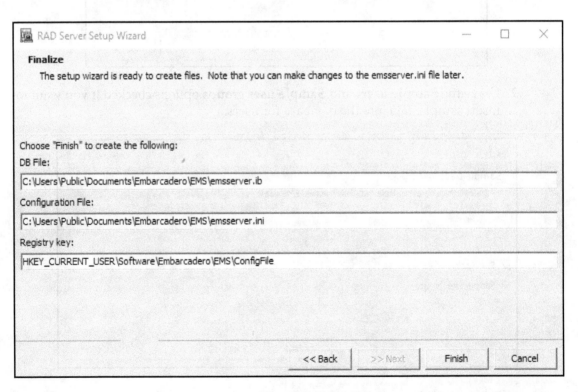

5. RAD Server is configured for development. The notice applies if necessary because the application in production will need to acquire a license. Click **Yes**:

By performing all the steps correctly, you will receive a confirmation from RAD Server stating that the installation/configuration was successful:

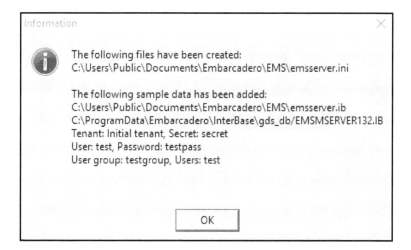

6. With our running test application, the first task we can take is to check whether the server is actually running:

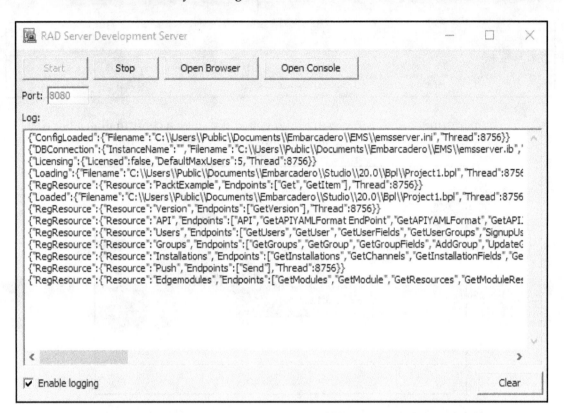

 Note that after running the project and proceeding with the initial configuration of RAD Server, the development console is active.

The development server has four functions, which are `Start`, `Stop`, `Open Browser`, and `Open Console`.

Note that as we begin our project, the server is already enabled. To perform another test, perform the following steps:

1. Click **Open Browser**:

   Note that the browser will load the URL: `localhost:8080/version`. This is the URL that will guarantee the status of the RAD Server service.

   Do you remember that at the beginning of the construction of this example, we inserted the value `PacktExample` for the name of the project?

2. Modify the URL: `localhost:8080/PackExample`. Now press *Enter*:

3. Stop program execution.
4. In order for you to understand how the `Get` method works, go back to the Delphi project and in the `TPacktExampleResource1.Get` procedure, and do the following:

```
procedure TPacktExampleResource1.Get(const AContext:
TEndpointContext; const ARequest: TEndpointRequest; const
AResponse: TEndpointResponse);
begin
  // Sample code
  AResponse.Body.SetValue(TJSONString.Create('This is a Get Method!
Packt Books Rocks!'), True)
end;
```

5. Start the project again using the **Play** button or the `F9` key.
6. Open the browser again.

7. Modify the URL: `localhost:8080/PackExample`. Now press *Enter*:

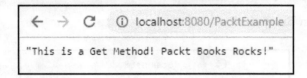

In all the preceding steps, we are working with the `PacktExample` resource; however, if I want to change this resource or add others, how can I do it? That's very simple. Let's change the `PacktExample` resource to `MyFirstRADServer`, by doing the following:

1. In the sample project, in the line that precedes the `TPacktExampleResource1` class, do the following:

```
type
  [ResourceName('MyFirstRADServer')] //change here
  TPacktExampleResource1 = class(TDataModule)
  published
    procedure Get(const AContext: TEndpointContext; const ARequest:
TEndpointRequest; const AResponse: TEndpointResponse);
    [ResourceSuffix('{item}')]
    procedure GetItem(const AContext: TEndpointContext; const
ARequest: TEndpointRequest; const AResponse: TEndpointResponse);
  end;
```

2. Run the application.
3. Open the browser by modifying the URL:
   `localhost:8080/MyFirstRADServer`:

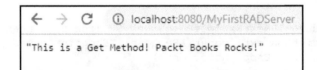

Note that once you modify the feature, it will be applied to the URL when you run it.

Consuming services on RAD Server

Now that you know the basics of microservices and know how RAD Server works, how about creating a server application, to consume a web service and then host this service in IIS (Windows)?

What we will do is create a RAD Server application that will query a currency conversion web service. Shall we begin?

To get started, start a new RAD Server project, just as you learned in the previous topic. Then, take the following steps:

1. Go to **Project** | **New** | **Other** | **RAD Server** | **RAD Server Package**:

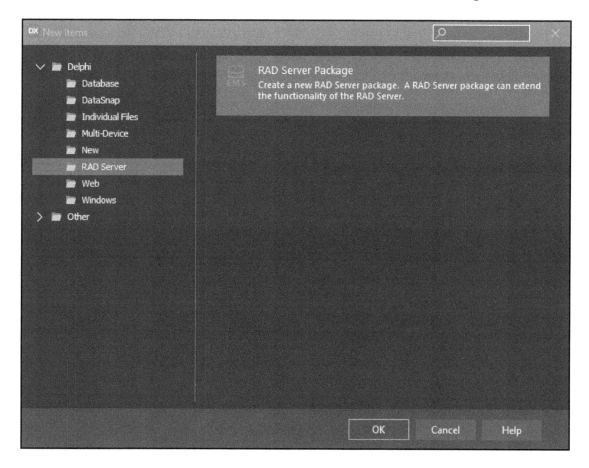

2. Create a package with resource.
3. Put the resource name as `Currency`.
4. Set the **File Type Data Module**.
5. Click on **Finish**.

RAD Server application

In the same way, as in the previous section, Delphi automatically created the unit by inserting the resource named `Currency`. Before programming money conversion, we first need to include the **Web Service Definition Language** (**WSDL**) of the web service we want to consume on RAD Server. The web service chosen for such a contract was `http://currencyconverter.kowabunga.net`.

To import the WSDL from the currency converter, first, we need to have the URL address of the web service in question.

Please follow these steps:

1. With your browser, open the `http://currencyconverter.kowabunga.net/converter.asmx` address.
2. You will see the site containing the list of SOAP API functions:

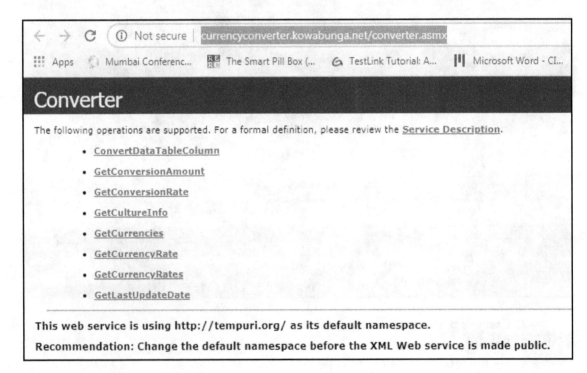

3. In the preceding screenshot, you will find the option to display the WSDL of the web service; click on the **Service Description** link.

4. You will be redirected to the page, containing the WSDL information. Copy the contents of the URL to the clipboard. The proposed URL is: `http://currencyconverter.kowabunga.net/converter.asmx?WSDL`.

5. Back in the Delphi IDE, the contents of the new URL will be copied to the clipboard. Open the Delphi WSDL importer by navigating to **File** | **New** | **Other** | **Web** | **WSDL Importer**:

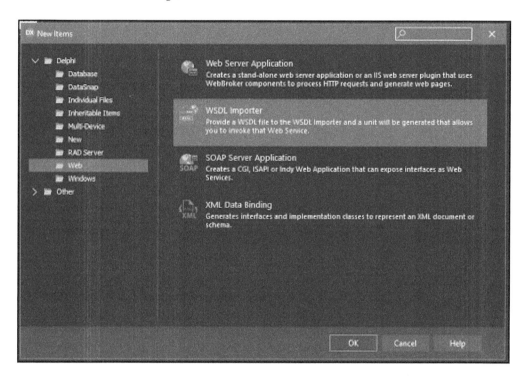

6. Enter the URL copied into the **WSDL Source** field:

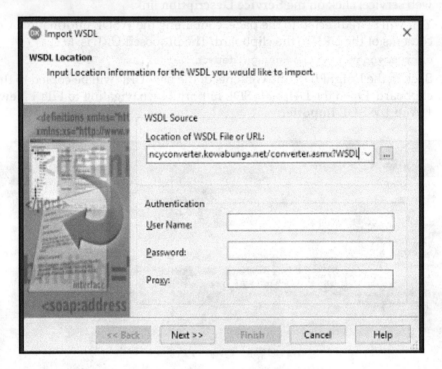

7. Advance through the next two screens and click **Finish** to load a new unit with the imported WSDL code.
8. Verify that Delphi imported a file called `convert.pas`. This file contains the imported WSDL code for consumption of the web service—currency converter.
9. Go back to **Unit1**, saving the project, and renaming **Unit1** to `uConverterRADServer.pas`.
10. Save the unit converter with the same name, only replacing the first letter with an uppercase letter.
11. Save the project name as `ConverterRS`.

12. Try to run the project. You will receive a prompt to enter new units. Click on **OK**:

This is the minimum we need now that RAD Server is up and running. We need to implement the call to the web service and capture the currency value we want and then return it to RAD Server in JSON format. In this case, as the conversion of the web service that we are consuming within a microservice in RAD Server is SOAP (converter), we will need some adapters to make everything work.

In our project, the goal is to ask the web service what the current quote is for a currency compared to the local currency. We will use as a test case the conversion of **United States Dollars (USD)** and **Brazilian Real (BRL)**.

To build web service consumption on RAD Server, follow these steps:

1. In the uses clause of the interface section, declare the following unit:

```
uses
   System.SysUtils, System.Classes, System.JSON,
   EMS.Services, EMS.ResourceAPI, EMS.ResourceTypes,
Soap.InvokeRegistry,
   Soap.Rio, Soap.SOAPHTTPClient, Converter;
```

2. Declare the following units, in the uses clause in the implementation section:

```
uses
   Xml.xmldom, Xml.omnixmldom, XSBuiltIns;
```

3. In the main class, `TCurrencyResource1`, add a public section containing the following property:

```
public
    property wsConverter : ConverterSoap read FwsConverter write
SetwsConverter;
```

4. Add a component of **HTTPRIO** type to the data module:

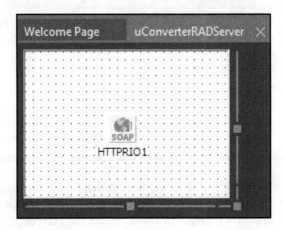

5. Configure the component with the WSDL server parameters that we consulted earlier:

6. First, fill out the **WSDLLocation**, and then select **Port** and **Service**.

7. In the **OnCreate** event of the data module, do the following:

```
procedure TCurrencyResource1.DataModuleCreate(Sender: TObject);
begin
  wsConverter := HTTPRIO1 as ConverterSoap;
end;
```

8. In the **OnDestroy** event, do this:

```
procedure TCurrencyResource1.DataModuleDestroy(Sender: TObject);
begin
  wsConverter := nil;
end;
```

Now that we have basically everything created and declared, we need to consume the SOAP API, returning its XML and turning its contents into a JSON value for the user.

9. Use the `GetItem` event to encode the following:

```
procedure TCurrencyResource1.GetItem(const AContext:
TEndpointContext; const ARequest: TEndpointRequest; const
AResponse: TEndpointResponse);
var
  LItem: string;
  Amount : TXSDecimal;
begin
  DefaultDOMVendor := sOmniXmlVendor;
  LItem := ARequest.Params.Values['item'];
  Amount := TXSDecimal.Create;
  Amount.DecimalString := LItem;

  AResponse.Body.SetValue(TJSONString.Create(
wsConverter.GetConversionAmount('USD','BRL',DateTimeToXSDateTime(Da
te-2),Amount).DecimalString ),True)
end;
```

Right from the start, we modified the default XML library for SOAP web service consumption. As we are working with a server without using co-class, we do not have support (unless we program) to MSXML, so we switched to the **Omni** library.

It is important to note that the data types, coming from WSDL, when being processed were created as `TXSDateTime` and `TXSDecimal`. These data types are XML SOAP. Notice that the `{item}` parameter will assume the value we want to convert; that is, the user will tell us how much to convert from USD to BRL.

Finally, we invoke the `GetConversionAmount` method of the web service that we are consuming, inserting the currency parameters (`USD` and `BRL`). The last `Date` parameter refers to the quotation from two days ago.

When executing and testing the following example, we will have the following result:

In the preceding example, USD 2,000 converted into just over BRL 7,800. Try other values.

Client application

Coding our client application is simpler than it appears to be. Leave an instance of your Delphi active, with the running RAD Server application, and follow these steps:

1. Open a new Delphi IDE, and start a new VCL project in **File** | **New** | **Windows VCL Application**:

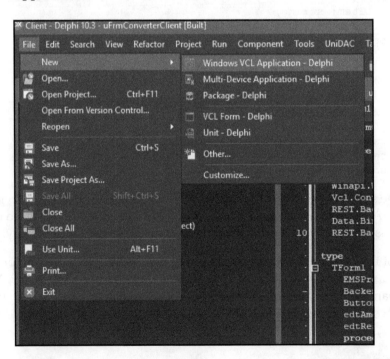

Let's add some visual components to the main form. Add the following components:

- A **TEdit**; rename it edtAmount.
- Other **TEdit**; rename it edtResult.
- A **TButton** component; rename it btnOK and put **Caption** as Convert.

2. For the nonvisual layer, that is, components that will not be displayed on the form at runtime, insert two components:

- Add **TEMSProvider** to the form.
- Add **TBackendEndPoint** to the form.

Your form should look something like this:

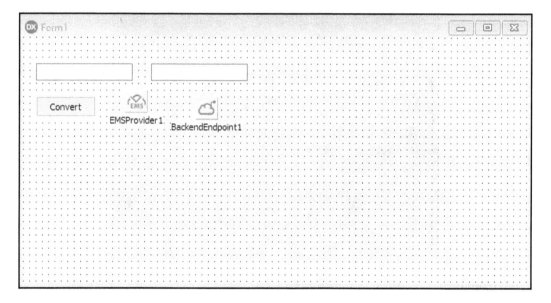

3. Now we need to configure the client provider to connect to RAD Server. Notice that we have only two components on the screen for this. Let's start with **EMSProvider1**. Modify the following properties:

- **URLHost** to localhost
- **URLPort** to 8080

This URL and port configuration refers to the physical address of RAD Server from which the connection is intended. In our example, RAD Server runs locally.

4. The last component that we will be setting is the **TBackendEndPoint**, which will define with what resource we are using the server. Modify the **Resource** property as currency:

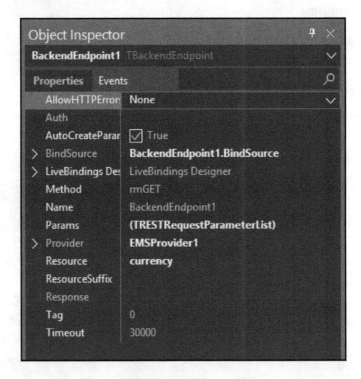

The two main components for connectivity to RAD Server, that we want for this example (return a simple JSON), is ready. Now we are missing the running of calls and the running of our tests. Please follow these steps:

1. Code the btnOK button:

```
procedure TForm1.btnOKClick(Sender: TObject);
begin
    BackendEndpoint1.ResourceSuffix := edtAmount.Text;
    BackendEndpoint1.Execute;
    edtResult.Text := BackendEndpoint1.Response.JSONText;
end;
```

The simplicity of Delphi is incredible. With a few lines of code, our client is ready to return the currency conversion.

2. Before finishing, follow the next steps to save the client project.

Are you reminding me that I asked you to leave your RAD Server project open so that we could develop in another instance of the IDE? Well, it's time to take the final test and consume your microservice:

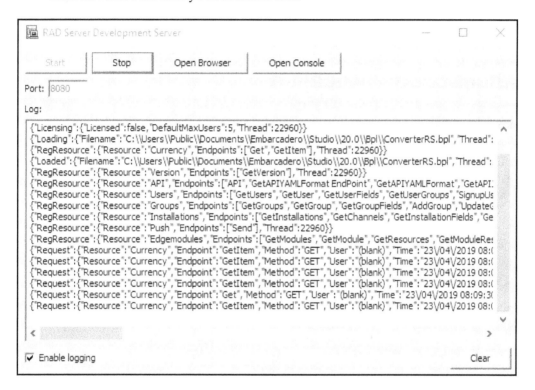

3. Run the program and make a call to our server:

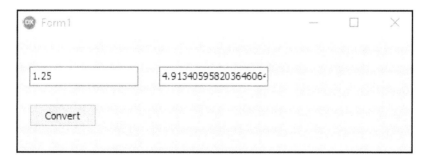

See that the call to our microservice is working, and our microservice does, in turn, perform the conversion web service perfectly. Cool, isn't it.

Security

Our microservice is somewhat vulnerable because anyone with the address and port can access it. To resolve this issue, we can include authentication, making our microservice more secure.

Authentication processes

Authentication is the process by which RAD Server requires your client applications to provide some identification beforehand to allow them to access their endpoints. By default, RAD Server comes with these settings disabled, just to facilitate the development and testing of the platform. However, in our case, we need to insert an authentication and that can be done in two ways:

- Application-level authentication
- Authentication at the user level

Application-level authentication

Application-level authentication requires that any client provide information before they can successfully request an endpoint.

RAD Server supports two types of authentication at the same application: `AppSecret` and the `MasterSecret`. They can be defined in the `Server.Keys` section of the RAD Server configuration INI file.

By default, the `AppSecret` value is empty in the `Server.Keys` section, but when the `AppSecret` value is set, the client must provide the `AppSecret` value in all resource requests to RAD Server. For this, it is enough that the clients pass the value of `AppSecret` in the header of the request through the `X-Embarcadero-App-Secret` parameter. When additional resource constraints are defined in the `Server.Authorization` section, both the `AppSecret` and the `Server.Authorization` constraints must be met concurrently.

This type of authentication is widely used for open applications and is very common when the user registers a new application when registering in a web tool.

By definition, you could also use the REST Library family component on the client side to consume a RAD Server service. In this case, using the authentication, as mentioned, you must load the X-Embarcadero-App-Secret parameter in the HTTP request header. When using RAD Server components, this process becomes transparent. Just configure it.

When the MasterSecret is defined and a client passes the value of MasterSecret in a request header, the rights to the requests are granted unconditionally. Specifically, any restrictions defined in the Server.Authorization section of the RAD Server configuration file is ignored when a valid MasterSecret is provided. Customers pass the value of MasterSecret in the request header through the X-Embarcadero-Master-Secret parameter.

 Once you have defined a MasterSecret for your RAD Server application, it will override any other existing security configuration. The MasterSecret function is only recommended for administrative users because it frees access to the entire application.

On Server.Keys, you will find one more option, the ApplicationID. ApplicationID does not apply specifically to authentication but can be used in installations where there are multiple RAD Servers to prevent a mismatch between the client and the server. Clients pass the value of the ApplicationID in the request header through the X-Embarcadero-Application-Id parameter. This setting is not closely linked to security or authentication but identifies the client applications and facilitates the consultation of RAD Server analysis.

User-level authentication

User-level authentication requires a user to formally log into the application to receive an access token. This session token is named X-Embarcadero-Session-Token in the configuration INI file and must be provided in the header of each request to enable the RAD Server to identify the user who logged in. This token is the authorization to the server.

This user-level authentication is integrated with RAD Server, where you can create groups or access profiles together with each user name. These users, when configured, will automatically belong to a group. Authentication by a user generates a token. When you enter a username and password, RAD Server will return you a token and this token should be used for all future calls.

Authentication and authorization

Authentication is the process of identifying a specific user. To authenticate a user, a client must first call the login or signup of the RAD Server administrative API user feature. Login is a POST request that passes a JSON object on the HTTP message body. This object must have two JSON properties, one of which is **username** and the other **password**. If the data supplied matches an existing RAD Server user, a session token is returned to the client in the response.

Authorization is the determination that a given user has the right to invoke a specific endpoint, and that can be done at the user or group level. A user- or group-level authorization is granted to allow or deny access to an endpoint or resource. In RAD Server, the control related to authorization and authentication is from the Server.Authorization section of the RAD Server configuration file.

> Signup is a feature that allows the user to self-register. This will authenticate too.

This is all the theoretical basis needed to proceed, now we can get our hands on and leave our microservice safe.

Implementation

If you do not remember, you can go back a few pages to the first run of the application and you will see the initial configuration of our development server. In it, when you confirm the information, a configuration INI file is saved to the disk, in addition to an InterBase database. If you have followed the steps correctly, your configuration file will be in the path: C:\Users\Public\Documents\Embarcadero\EMS\emsserver.ini:

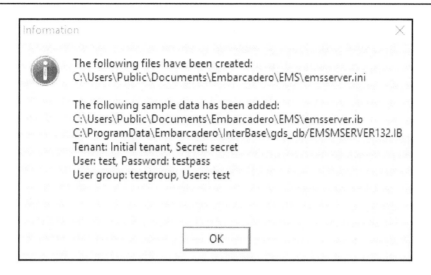

Let's do a little test. Follow the next steps:

1. Open the `emsserver.ini` file.

2. In the `[Server.Keys]` section, change the `AppSecret` key to `Packt` and save it:

```
 1   [Data]
 2   ;# Interbase connection parameters
 3   InstanceName=
 4   Database=C:\Users\Public\Documents\Embarcadero\EMS\emsserver.ib
 5   UserName=sysdba
 6   Password=masterkey
 7   SEPassword=
 8   ;# SEPassword connects to an encrypted database
 9   Pooled=
10   ;# Set Pooled=0 to disable connection pooled, Pooled=1 to enable. Default value is 1.
11   PooledMax=
12   ;# Set PooledMax=10 to limit maximum pooled connection.  Default value is 50.
13
14   [Server.Limits]
15   MaxConnections=
16   ;# Set MaxConnections=10 to limit maximum concurrent HTTP requests.  Default is 32.
17   MaxUsers=
18   ;# Set MaxUsers=3 to limit the number of users in the EMS database.  This value is only used
19   ;# when less than the maximum users permitted by the EMS runtime license.
20
21   [Server.Keys]
22   MasterSecret=
23   ;# MasterSecret may be blank.  If blank then the EMS server will not support
24   ;# MasterSecret authentication.
25   ;# HTTP 401 (Unauthorized) is raised if a request contains an incorrect MasterSecret
26   AppSecret=Packt
27   ;# AppSecret may be blank.  If AppSecret is not blank all requests must include the AppSecret.
28   ;# HTTP 401 (Unauthorized) is raised if a request does not contain a correct AppSecret
29   ApplicationID=
30   ;# ApplicationID may be blank.  If ApplicationID is not blank, all requests must include the ApplicationID.
31   ;# HTTP 404 (not found) is raised if a request does not contain a correct ApplicationID
```

3. Go back to the application's built-in RAD Server and let it run; you do not need to change anything.

4. Run your client application, the same one that we built earlier, and click the button to convert a value:

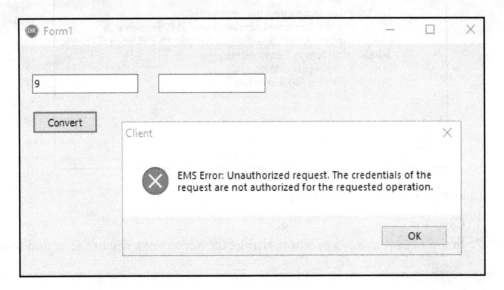

Notice that the change to the configuration file has already taken effect. The same goes for the other options in the Server.Keys section. To resolve this issue, do the following:

1. In the client application, go to the **EMSProvider1** component and change the **AppSecret** property to Packt:

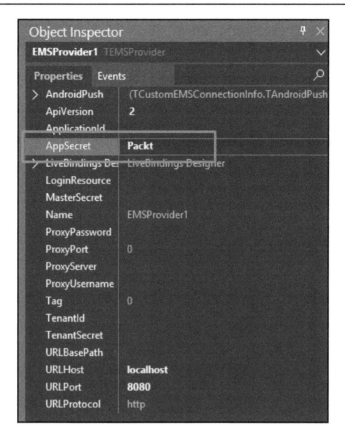

2. Please retry and test again:

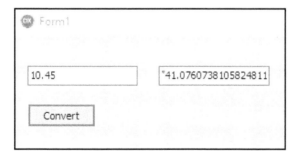

Our application is almost fully secure. We have made the authorization through the keys in the `Server.Keys` section of the RAD Server configuration file, and now we will complete the security part, it lacks the authentication of the users. When you first configure RAD Server, a test user is created as we left it checked in the initial configuration.

If you need to include more groups and users, an easy and quick way to resolve this is through the `EMSManagementConsole.exe` application that is available in the same directory as the RAD Server. Let's introduce the default user and password and create a new one. To do this, follow these steps:

1. Go to the root directory of the RAD Server, at `C:\Program Files (x86)\Embarcadero\Studio\20.0\bin`.
2. Open `EMSManagementConsole.exe`.
3. Go to **Profile | New Profile**:

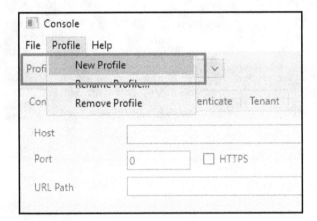

4. On the **Connection** tab, enter the server data, such as **Host**: `localhost` and **Port**: `8080`.
5. Click **Connect**. You can see that an authorization error occurs. This is due to the fact that we have previously defined an **AppSecret**. Go to the **Keys** tab and put `Packt` as **AppSecret**:

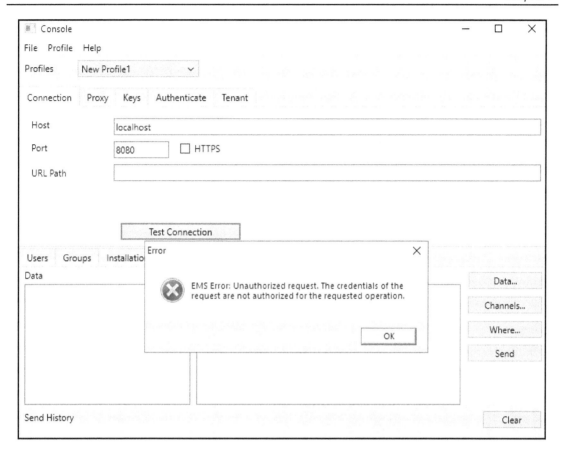

6. After adding the correct value to **AppSecret**, try connecting, by clicking on **Test Connection**.

7. Once logged in, we can now authenticate with the testing user to then have access to the user control. In the **Authenticate** tab, define the following fields for the user:

- **User name**: test
- **Password**: testpass as shown in the following screenshot:

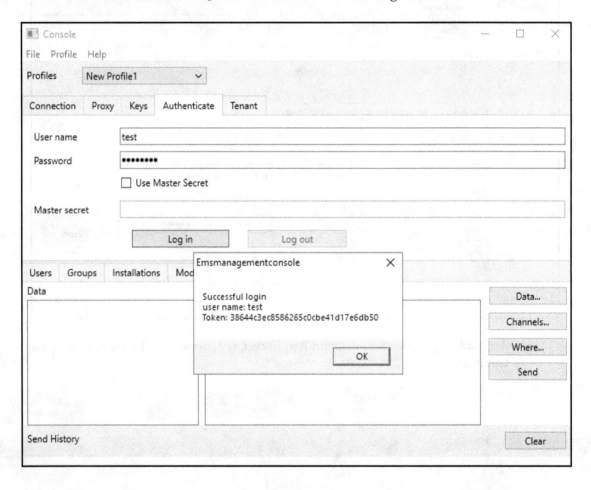

8. Being logged in, authenticated, and authorized, you can browse between groups, users, and other tabs. Save this user number and password and let the `emsserver.ini` file make a small change and save it:

```
[Server.Authorization]
currency={"groups": ["testgroup"]}
```

9. Back in the client application, add the following components to the main form:

   • Two **TEdits**, one with the **password char** property with the value of *.
   • Add a **TButton** component and change the **Name** property to `btnLogin`.
   • Add a **TBackendAuth** component as shown in the following screenshot:

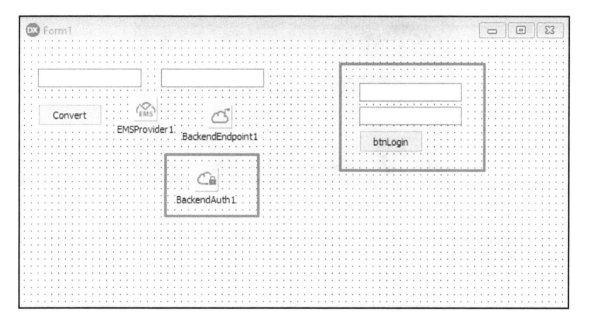

10. Go to the **BackendEndpoint1** component and modify the **Auth** property by setting the value for the new **BackendAuth1** component added:

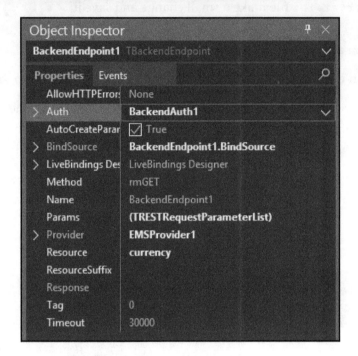

11. Finally, code the **onClick** event of the `btnLogin` button:

```
procedure TForm1.btnLoginClick(Sender: TObject);
begin
  BackendAuth1.UserName := Edit1.Text;
  BackendAuth1.Password := edit2.Text;
  BackendAuth1.Login;
  if BackendAuth1.LoggedIn then
    ShowMessage('Success');
end;
```

12. Save and run the client. Make sure the server is running:

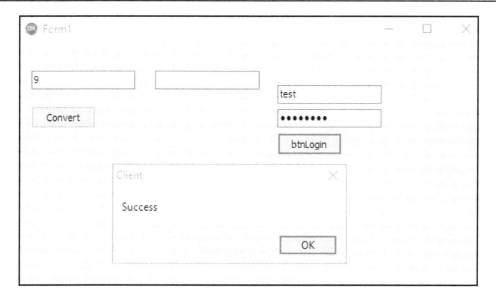

Now the application is secure, and only authenticated and authorized users can perform queries.

However, if I need this control of users and groups outside of my configuration file, having the checks inside the server's own executable is also possible.

In the server application, go to the GetItem event and code as follows:

```
procedure TCurrencyResource1.GetItem(const AContext: TEndpointContext;
const ARequest: TEndpointRequest; const AResponse: TEndpointResponse);
var
  LItem: string;
  Amount : TXSDecimal;
begin
  if AContext.User = nil then
    EEMSHTTPError.RaiseUnauthorized('', 'User Required');
  if not AContext.User.Groups.Contains('testgroup') then
    EEMSHTTPError.RaiseForbidden('','Test Group Required');

  DefaultDOMVendor := sOmniXmlVendor;
  LItem := ARequest.Params.Values['item'];
  Amount := TXSDecimal.Create;
  Amount.DecimalString := LItem;

  AResponse.Body.SetValue(TJSONString.Create(
wsConverter.GetConversionAmount('USD','BRL',DateTimeToXSDateTime(Date-2),Am
ount).DecimalString ),True)
end;
```

Note that when you start the `GetItem` method, we look for the connected user in the `AContext` variable of type `TEndpointContext`. If a user is not logged in, then an exception will be thrown, and then another test to see if the user, although authenticated, has permission. Here, we test with `TestGroup`; however, you can create your own users and groups.

What is missing now? How about performing the deployment of our server? This is what we will see in the next topic.

Deployment

Finally, we can do the deployment in production of our microservice. However, it is important to point out once again that you will need a single or multiproduction site license to install your application on IIS.

In this final part of the chapter, I will not address the IIS installation; however, I assume you already have IIS enabled on your Windows. If this is news to you, I leave a complete tutorial with step-by-step guidance to install/enable IIS on your computer in the following section.

Deployment on IIS

You can check the following links for the step-by-step installation of IIS on your operating system:

- **Install IIS on Windows 8 (this also works for Windows 10):** `https://www.howtogeek.com/112455/how-to-install-iis-8-on-windows-8/`
- **Install IIS on Windows Server:** `https://docs.microsoft.com/en-us/iis/get-started/whats-new-in-iis-8/installing-iis-8-on-windows-server-2012`

RAD Server uses the InterBase server as a database management system to store its internal information, such as users, groups, access data, analyses, statistics, and so on. In this step, even though you have an InterBase installed, you must create a new installation with a distinguished instance name. Otherwise, you will not be able to run and deploy your application.

If you don't have a license for InterBase you can download a trial version at `https://www.embarcadero.com/products/interbase/start-for-free`.

After you download InterBase, proceed with the installation. It is important to note that if you already have InterBase for development on the machine, RAD Server will only work if you install InterBase with a different name on the instance and on another port:

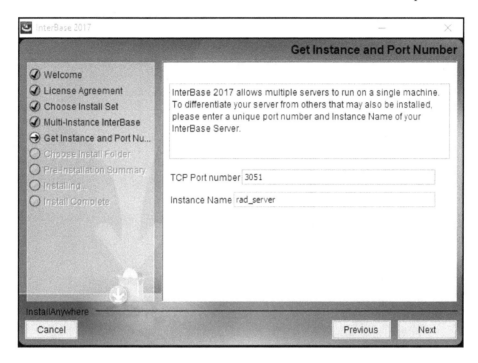

In this installation, for example, InterBase is installed on port `3051` with the `rad_server` instance name.

 If you already have a functional RAD Server license, you do not need to reinstall it. You can copy the settings.

With InterBase installed on a new instance and enabled, you need to configure IIS.

To do this, follow these steps:

1. Open `localhost` at your browser to know whether IIS is working:

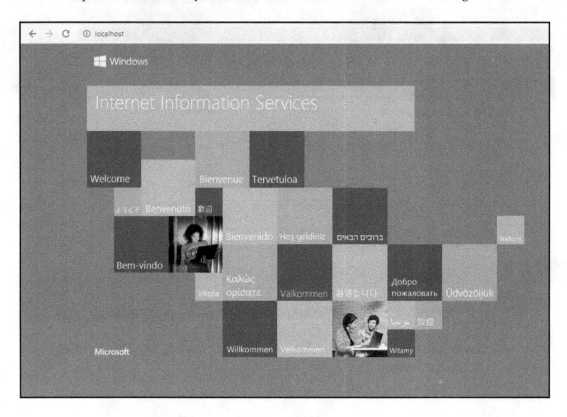

2. Navigate to the default IIS directory: `C:\inetpub\wwwroot`.
3. Create a new folder inside `inetpub`, called `packtserver`.
4. Open IIS and in the default website, right-click and select **Add new virtual directory**.
5. Fill in the **Alias** with the `packtserver` name as the folder you created.
6. On the physical path, select the created folder: `C:\inetpub\wwwroot\packtserver`.
7. Repeat the same process and create a second folder, also in the `c:\inetpub\wwwroot` root, called `packtconsole`, to save the console information:

This should be your folder structure in the path `C:\inetpub\wwwroot\`:

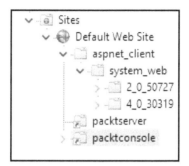

The virtual directories in IIS should also be as shown in the preceding screenshot.

8. Copy the following files from the `C:\Program Files (x86)\Embarcadero\Studio\20.0\bin` folder to the `C:\inetpub\wwwroot\packtserver`:

- `borlndmm.dll`
- `CustomIPTransport260.bpl`
- `dbrtl260.bpl`
- `EMSConsole.dll`
- `EMSServer.dll`
- `emsserverapi260.bpl`
- `FireDAC260.bpl`
- `FireDACCommon260.bpl`
- `FireDACCommonDriver260.bpl`
- `rtl260.bpl`
- `FireDACIBDriver260.bpl`
- `IndyCore260.bpl`

- IndyIPClient260.bpl
- IndyIPCommon260.bpl
- IndyProtocols260.bpl
- IndySystem260.bpl
- inet260.bpl
- xmlrtl260.bpl

This list of dependencies is the default RAD Server, that is, the minimum that RAD Server needs to run in IIS. If your microservices use other BPLs, you should copy your dependencies to the folder as well.

You need to create a RAD Server database using your license (this database will be encrypted). The most practical way to do this is to use EMSDevServer.exe itself, located in C:\Program Files (x86)\Embarcadero\Studio\20.0\bin. You can copy the EMSDevServer.exe to a new folder in your server, along with the dependency files that you have already copied previously for the EMSServer.dll deployment. You also need to copy the template files to the new database creation. These files are located in the C:\Program Files (x86)\Embarcadero\Studio\20.0\ObjRepos\en\EMS folder.

Create a folder named ObjRepos at the same level as the EMSDevServer.exe folder, and then copy the entire EMS directory into the newly created ObjRepos folder.

If you want to work with the RAD Server x64 bits, you can copy the dependencies of the bin64 folder, while your applications should also be compiled in 64 bits.

Please follow the next steps carefully:

1. In IIS, select the virtual packtserver directory and go to the **Handler Mappings** option:

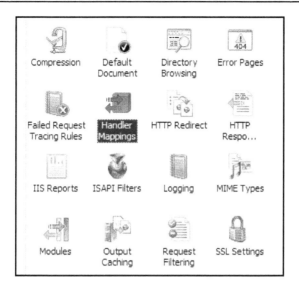

2. Select **Edit Feature Permissions ...** in the **Actions** panel.

3. Check **Execute** and save:

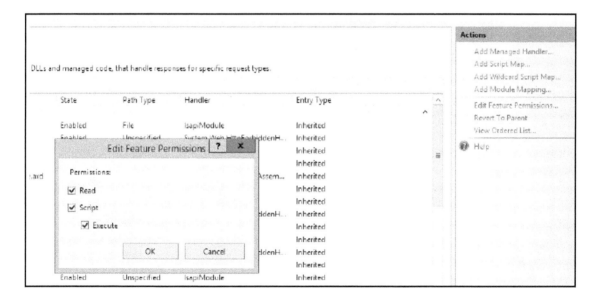

4. Select the **ISAPI-dll** handler item.
5. Enter the correct location of the EMSServer.dll application:

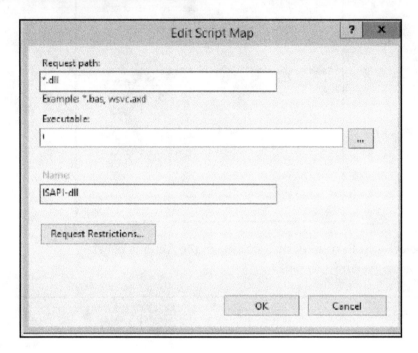

6. Repeat the steps for the PacktConsole directory.
7. When you enter the location of the DLL in the PacktConsole folder, enter the EMSConsole.dll file.
8. Copy emsserver.ini from the default location C:\Users\Public\Documents\Embarcadero\EMS\ to the IIS Packtserver directory:

borlndmm.dll	04/02/2019 21:55	Extensão de aplica...	69 KB
CustomIPTransport260.bpl	04/02/2019 21:55	Arquivo BPL	220 KB
dbrtl260.bpl	04/02/2019 21:55	Arquivo BPL	671 KB
EMSConsole.dll	04/02/2019 21:55	Extensão de aplica...	7.350 KB
EMSServer.dll	04/02/2019 21:55	Extensão de aplica...	4.215 KB
emsserver	24/04/2019 01:22	Parâmetros de co...	9 KB
emsserverapi260.bpl	04/02/2019 21:55	Arquivo BPL	904 KB
FireDAC260.bpl	04/02/2019 21:55	Arquivo BPL	870 KB
FireDACCommon260.bpl	04/02/2019 21:55	Arquivo BPL	979 KB
FireDACCommonDriver260.bpl	04/02/2019 21:55	Arquivo BPL	866 KB
FireDACIBDriver260.bpl	04/02/2019 21:55	Arquivo BPL	398 KB
IndyCore260.bpl	04/02/2019 21:55	Arquivo BPL	399 KB
IndyIPClient260.bpl	04/02/2019 21:55	Arquivo BPL	68 KB
IndyIPCommon260.bpl	04/02/2019 21:55	Arquivo BPL	69 KB
IndyProtocols260.bpl	04/02/2019 21:55	Arquivo BPL	2.588 KB
IndySystem260.bpl	04/02/2019 21:55	Arquivo BPL	310 KB
inet260.bpl	04/02/2019 21:55	Arquivo BPL	296 KB
rtl260.bpl	04/02/2019 21:55	Arquivo BPL	12.691 KB
web	24/04/2019 00:09	Embarcadero RAD...	1 KB

9. Open the `emsserver.ini` file from the IIS `Packtserver` directory and change the following keys:

```
[Data]
;# InterBase connection parameters
InstanceName=rad_sever
Database=C:\Users\Public\Documents\Embarcadero\EMS
```

Change the following key:

```
[Server.Connection.Dev]
Port=80
```

The following screenshot depicts the changes made to the keys:

```
emsserver.ini
 1    [Data]
 2    ;# Interbase connection parameters
 3    InstanceName=rad_server
 4    Database=C:\Users\Public\Documents\Embarcadero\EMS
 5    UserName=sysdba
 6    Password=masterkey
 7    SEPassword=
 8    ;# SEPassword connects to an encrypted database
 9    Pooled=
10    ;# Set Pooled=0 to disable connection pooled, Pooled=1 to enable. Default value is 1.
11    PooledMax=
12    ;# Set PooledMax=10 to limit maximum pooled connection.  Default value is 50.
13
14    [Server.Limits]
15    MaxConnections=
16    ;# Set MaxConnections=10 to limit maximum concurrent HTTP requests.  Default is 32.
17    MaxUsers=
18    ;# Set MaxUsers=3 to limit the number of users in the EMS database.  This value is only used
19    ;# when less than the maximum users permitted by the EMS runtime license.
20
21    [Server.Keys]
22    MasterSecret=
23    ;# MasterSecret may be blank.  If blank then the EMS server will not support
24    ;# MasterSecret authentication.
25    ;# HTTP 401 (Unauthorized) is raised if a request contains an incorrect MasterSecret
26    AppSecret=
27    ;# AppSecret may be blank.  If AppSecret is not blank all requests must include the AppSecret.
28    ;# HTTP 401 (Unauthorized) is raised if a request does not contain a correct AppSecret
29    ApplicationID=
30    ;# ApplicationID may be blank.  If ApplicationID is not blank, all requests must include the ApplicationID.
31    ;# HTTP 404 (not found) is raised if a request does not contain a correct ApplicationID
32
33    [Server.Connection.Dev]
34    Port=80
35    ;# The following options enable HTTPS support.
```

10. Copy `emsserver.ini` from the `Packserver` folder to the `PacktConsole` folder.

11. Change `emsserver.ini` in the `packtconsole` folder:

```
[Console.Paths.ISAPI]
ResourcesFiles= C:\inetpub\wwwroot\packtconsole\
```

Make the modifications according to the directory and instance that you will use for the server. In our case, we have a second instance called `rad_server`. The change from port `8080` to port `80` is to work directly in IIS without the need to change the port because port `80` is the internet standard.

And, finally, restart the IIS server, and then call the URL: `http://localhost/packtserver/emsserver.dll/version`.

In this case, my license is developmental only, so I will not have the EMS version in the browser. The message that will appear in the following screenshot:

To purchase a license, simply contact Embarcadero in your country.

It is possible that you will use the server and x86-bit DLLs. If you are working with x86-bit architecture, you need to configure the IIS application pool to work with this architecture. The required setting is established as follows:

1. Click the application pool's node.
2. Click **DefaultAppPool** item.
3. Click **Advanced Settings ...** from the **Actions** panel.
4. An **Advanced Settings** dialog opens.
5. Set **Enable 32-Bits Applications** to True.
6. Click **OK**:

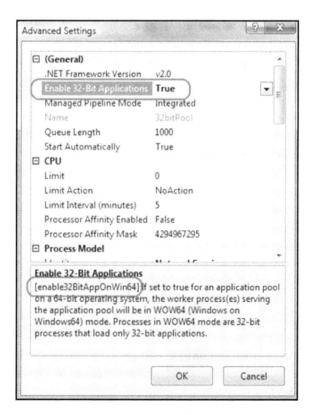

Thus, you can distribute your applications in the cloud and take advantage of all the features of IIS.

Summary

Congratulations! Thank you for getting here. Our last and longest chapter in this book has addressed the concepts of microservices and how to work with them using RAD Server.

At the beginning of the chapter, you learned a little about microservice architecture and what it is, and what a monolithic application consists of. Now think about how the knowledge gained in this chapter can help you modularize your applications and empower your users.

Faced with this scenario, factors such as scalability, performance, availability, and productivity are important points to consider when building an application. In order to achieve that end, these concepts have been discussed and new ways of organizing computer systems have been put into practice, leaving aside traditional forms of developing an application, as is the case with monolithic applications, whose profiles do not always fit into this current perspective.

In the course of the chapter, you learned how to configure a RAD Server development server for either 32 or 64 bits. The path will be the same, changing only the executables. InterBase installation was required to follow up the tasks, if it was not done at the time you installed RAD Studio.

Next, we created a microservice capable of consuming a web service built using SOAP technology and returning it to the REST client. But our application was insecure; that is, anyone could consume our micro service without the slightest problem.

Advancing to the security side, we introduced the concept of authentication and authorization and examined the differences between each. We can work with either of them or both. The possibilities are enormous, from changing an INI file, to encoding the rules of authentication and authorization in the microservice itself.

At the end of the chapter, something was missing—And now? How can my microservice built under RAD Server be published? After you installed IIS, you saw how to configure and enable ISAPI filters so that the EMS server could run. A good tip is that if you work with x86-bit architecture, you can modify the default application pool for x86-bit support.

We have come to the end of another chapter and also the end of the book. I am very happy to have had you here with me on this journey, dear reader. Thank you very much, and see you next time!

Further reading

For more information, you can check out the following links:

- **RAD Server and Beacon Fence at Saitobaru Museum**: https://www.youtube.com/watch?v=fdOt9-K8oTQ
- **RAD Server, The Perfect Back-end for your Apps**: https://youtu.be/HY0JRJPvjsU
- **Beyond The Beacon Fence**: https://youtu.be/1_cWnDmvxJk
- **Beacon Fencing con RAD Studio, Delphi y C++Builder**: https://youtu.be/bJG4UEjuMeM
- **Using the Wahoo Digital Scale ThingConnect IoT component in your Delphi Apps**: https://youtu.be/tQlYAlvfpPQ
- **RAD Server Nurse Station Demo**: https://www.youtube.com/watch?v=TFK6tJoI78A
- **ThingPoint Overview**: http://docwiki.embarcadero.com/RADStudio/Rio/en/ThingPoints_Overview
- **ThingConnect**: http://docwiki.embarcadero.com/IoT/en/ThingConnect
- **ThingConnect Devices**: http://docwiki.embarcadero.com/IoT/en/ThingConnect_Devices
- **IoT Edgeware**: https://goo.gl/rO2528

Other Books You May Enjoy

If you enjoyed this book, you may be interested in these other books by Packt:

Hands-On Design Patterns with Delphi
Primož Gabrijelčič

ISBN: 9781789343243

- Gain insights into the concept of design patterns
- Study modern programming techniques with Delphi
- Keep up to date with the latest additions and program design techniques in Delphi
- Get to grips with various modern multithreading approaches
- Discover creational, structural, behavioral, and concurrent patterns
- Determine how to break a design problem down into its component parts

Delphi Cookbook - Third Edition
Daniele Spinetti, Daniele Teti

ISBN: 9781788621304

- Develop visually stunning applications using FireMonkey
- Deploy LiveBinding effectively with the right object-oriented programming (OOP) approach
- Create RESTful web services that run on Linux or Windows
- Build mobile apps that read data from a remote server efficiently
- Call platform native API on Android and iOS for an unpublished API
- Manage software customization by making better use of an extended RTTI
- Integrate your application with IOT

Leave a review - let other readers know what you think

Please share your thoughts on this book with others by leaving a review on the site that you bought it from. If you purchased the book from Amazon, please leave us an honest review on this book's Amazon page. This is vital so that other potential readers can see and use your unbiased opinion to make purchasing decisions, we can understand what our customers think about our products, and our authors can see your feedback on the title that they have worked with Packt to create. It will only take a few minutes of your time, but is valuable to other potential customers, our authors, and Packt. Thank you!

Index

photos
    sharing, FireMonkey used 24, 25

R

RAD Server
    about 180, 181, 182
    application 194, 197, 198, 199, 200
    client application 200, 201, 202, 203
    configuring 183, 184, 185, 186, 187, 191, 192
    services, consuming 192, 193
remote control
    building, project overview 156
remote service 75
repositories
    about 97
    PostgreSQL repository 110, 112, 113, 116
    singleton 118, 123
    SQL Server repository 98, 100, 101, 105
Representational State Transfer (REST) 29
responsive layouts
    creating 12
    TLayout 13
REST services
    requesting 34
    response 34
    working 35

S

Scalable Vector Graphics (SVG) 7
screens
    data, sending from mobile to desktop 161, 163,
      164, 165, 166, 167, 168, 169
    sharing 161
security
    about 204

application-level authentication 204, 205
authentication 206
authentication processes 204
authorization 206
implementing 206, 208, 210, 212, 213, 214,
  216
user-level authentication 205, 206
Service Control Manager (SCM) 56
service-oriented architecture (SOA) 177
Simple Object Access Protocol (SOAP) 180
singleton 119
Software as a Service (SaaS) 177

T

TLayout 13
TMultiView
    using 136, 140

U

Uniform Resource Identifier (URI) 41
United States Dollars (USD) 197
user-level authentication 205, 206
username 206

W

Web Service Definition Language (WSDL) 194
WebView 33
Windows services
    creating 50, 51, 53, 55
    debugging 61
    installing 55, 58
    service threads 62
    starting 59
    stopping 59
    uninstalling 55, 58

* 9 7 8 1 7 8 9 1 3 0 5 5 3 *